Three Generations

Three Generations

Riding the Waves of Change in Your Church

Gary L. McIntosh

Fleming H. Revell
A Division of Baker Book House Co
Grand Rapids, Michigan 49516

Published by Fleming H. Revell
a division of Baker Book House Company
P.O. Box 6287, Grand Rapids, MI 49516-6287

Printed in the United States of America

Library of Congress Cataloging-in-Publication Data

McIntosh, Gary, 1947–
Three generations : riding the waves of change in your church / Gary L. McIntosh.
p. cm.
Includes bibliographical references.
ISBN 0-8007-5544-8
1. Church work. 2. Christianity—United States—21st century. 3. Church work with the aged. 4. Church work with the baby boom generation. 5. United States—Religion—1960– I. Title.
BV4403.M37 1995
250'.973—dc20 94-44012

Dedicated to the Builders in my life:

My grandmother, Wilma Thompson, who faithfully read the Bible in my presence as I was growing up and gave me my first knowledge of God and his church.

My mother, Billie C. McIntosh, who sacrificially gave me everything she never had as a child growing up in the Great Depression and constantly encouraged me in my education and ministry.

My father- and mother-in-law, Bill and Amelia Kurylow, who loved me as their own son and entrusted me with their daughter.

Nelle Roberts and David and Gladys Bishop, faithful servants of our Lord who introduced me to Jesus Christ as my Lord and Savior.

Rev. Erwin and Wilna Ericson, who taught me the Word of God and gave me my first opportunities to serve Christ.

Rev. Bob and Louise Duggan, who put up with my youthful exuberance and helped polish my rough edges.

Rev. Dennis and Shirley Perkins, co-laborers in the faith who befriended me as a young seminary student and helped me gain confidence as a pastor.

Contents

Waves of Change 9

Part 1: The Builder Wave

1 What Shaped the Builders? 25
2 Builders and the Church 44
3 Elderly Builders 56

Part 2: The Boomer Wave

4 Who Are the Boomers? 73
5 Boomer Believers 93
6 Reaching the Boomer Generation 107

Part 3: The Buster Wave

7 Why Are They Called Busters? 129
8 Busters and the Church 144
9 Reaching Busters 153

Part 4: Riding the Waves of Change

10 Blending Generations 171
11 Undercurrents of Discontent 184
12 Wave Runners 194

Notes 205
Resources 211
The McIntosh Church Growth Network 215

Lord, Thou hast been our dwelling place in all generations.

Psalm 90:1

Waves of Change

Scripture uses the word *generation* in three different ways. It can be an age group in a family, a period of time, or a group of people connected by their place in time. The genealogical tables found in Genesis and Matthew are obvious examples of the first. When the Psalmist writes, "I will cause Thy name to be remembered in all generations" (Ps. 45:17), he could have said "in all times" or "in all ages," which is an example of the second. However, the third definition is what I am thinking of in *Three Generations: Riding the Waves of Change in Your Church.* A generation is a group of people who are connected by their place in time with common boundaries and a common character.

The study of generational change has been an important aspect of my life since 1983. In July of that year I left a seven-year pastorate to become vice president of consulting services for Dr. Win Arn at the Institute for American Church Growth, then located in Pasadena, California.

Shortly after I arrived, one of my fellow consultants, Rev. Robert Orr, shared some thoughts he had on the baby boom generation and their impact on churches. The interest he created was intensified about one year later while I was traveling by airplane to a consulting assignment in New Jersey.

While on the plane, I found a November 5, 1984, copy of *U.S. News & World Report* and began reading its major article "Here Come the Baby Boomers." When I finished reading that article, I was hooked. For the past twelve years, I've read, clipped, and filed just about every article I could find on generational issues. I honestly don't know how many articles I've collected, but the file that contains them is more than three feet thick.

In 1986 I became associate professor of practical theology at Talbot School of Theology (Biola University), where I teach courses on church growth, evangelism, and leadership. The study of generational change has continued to be one of my prime interests, and being a professor has given me the opportunity to pursue it. During the past twelve years, I've spoken on generational change at denominational conferences, local churches, and seminars. I've also written several articles on the topic.

Why Another Book on Generations?

There were very few books on the topic of Baby Boomers in 1983 and none on Baby Busters. Today as I review the books available I can easily name more than fifty.

Of the collection of books I have on generations, most are on the Boomers. Some are secular books such as Paul C. Light's groundbreaking *Baby Boomers.* Others focus on the challenge Boomers bring to the church, such as Doug Murren's *The Baby Boomerang.* Still others, like Cheryl Russell's *100 Predictions for the Baby Boom,* offer insights on the future of the Boomer Generation.

Today new books, such as William Dunn's *The Baby Bust: A Generation Comes of Age* and Steven Gibb's *Twentysomething, Floundering, and Off the Yuppie Track,* are addressing the uniqueness of the Buster Generation.

Generational change has become quite a popular topic, and the book that seemed to start it all was Ken Dychtwald's *Age Wave.* This book alerted people to the aging of America. Two years later, William Strauss and Neil Howe released their massive study, *Generations: The History of America's Future 1584 to 2069.* It has been reviewed and quoted in numerous publications and will likely form the foundation for future studies on the issue.

My interest in generational issues, however, goes much deeper than a mere intellectual study. I've often felt a special kinship with Timothy, who was raised by his grandmother Lois and his mother, Eunice (2 Tim. 1:5). I, too, was raised by my grandmother and my mother. Ours was a multigenerational home—my grandmother was born in 1896, my mother was born in 1923, and I'm an older Boomer. Generational issues were always a topic of discussion in our home, and I continue to have a concern that generations work together.

As I've traveled, consulting with churches and leading church growth seminars during the past twelve years, I've noticed that most churches target one generation exclusively—Builders or Boomers or Busters—while often ignoring the others. Most books and articles on the topic also seem to target a single generation without including all three generational groups.

As pastors and church leaders, most of us don't have the choice of working with only one generation. In most of our churches all generations are present, and we must build a ministry that includes them all.

That is why I've written *Three Generations.* While I certainly do not have all of the answers, I believe this book will assist pastors, church leaders, and laypersons to keep all three generations in view and gain some insights into ways to integrate the generations for effective ministry.

The Panoramic Approach

As I contemplated writing this book, I was faced with two possible approaches. I could write the book with a microscopic view, attempting to cover every detail, aspect, and nuance of each generation. Or I could write the book with more of a panoramic view, presenting the larger picture with a few aspects of each generation standing out like trees in a landscape.

I've chosen to take the panoramic approach, and thus broad generalizations about each generation should be expected. There are aspects of each generation that may not be highlighted as much as some may wish. I have not delved into the differences that minorities or various ethnic groups might encounter. Nor have I touched on the differences created by geography, education, or economic conditions. In most cases, however, the generalizations suggested will fit about three-fourths of the members of the generation.

It is my hope that you will be able to identify enough with the insights suggested that you will gain a better understanding of the issues involved in ministering to multiple generational groups in your church. Working together in love is a key aspect of a healthy church (John 13:34–35).

Three Generational Waves

If you had to put everyone in the United States into three groups, how would you do it? On what basis would you group them? Would you use geographic location, educational background, income level, or entertainment preferences as determining factors? It would depend on your purpose.

If you had to put everyone in your church into three groups, how would you divide them? Since your purpose is ministry, finding common denominators for the people in your congregation could help you minister to them more effectively.

Certain people in your congregation are connected by a place in time, by common boundaries, and by a common character. We can say that those people are of one generation. Their ages may vary widely, but they tend to identify with each other because of national or world events they've all experienced, fads they've enjoyed, or prominent people they've come to know. They tend to share certain character traits or characteristics that reflect their time in history. The group is loosely held together by these experiential threads and by some common beliefs. They do some things in ways unique to the group, and they tend to see differences between themselves and members of other groups.

As we study American society today, we see that there are groups of people with shared characteristics and similar interests. We can fit most people into three broad groups.

Those who range in age from the late forties and up can be called the Builders; the Boomers are those in their early thirties to late forties; and children of about twelve years old through young adults in their twenties are the Busters.

As a generation moves through time, it causes a generational wave. Many members of a group will move through childhood, young adulthood, midlife, and retirement as a group, although the youngest and oldest members of the group will experience these phases at different times. As the group moves along it creates changes or waves that are identified specifically with that generation. The larger the generation, the larger the wave it creates.

Ever since the beginning of the twentieth century, Americans have been fond of placing labels on groups of people that influence our culture. Remember these? Bobby-soxers (1940s), Beatniks (1950s), Hippies (1960s), Preppies (1970s), and Valley Girls (1980s).

The influence of most of these groups was fairly small. They created little more than a stirring up of the sand on the beaches of change. However, when the Boomer wave between 1946 and 1964 crashed against the shores of change, we all took notice.

The Boomer wave is a generation bounded by the end of World War II and the decline of the high birth rate beginning in 1965. (Nineteen sixty-four was the last year with a birth rate of more than 4 million.) These boundaries set this generation apart from past generations and those that would follow. Like a tidal wave, we measure all other waves against it, particularly the waves just before and after it: the Builder wave and the Buster wave.[1]

The Boomer Wave

The Boomer Generation is the largest and most studied generation in U.S. history. It comprises two major groups: the Leading-Edge Boomers (LEBs) and the Trailing-Edge Boomers (TREBs). Influential members of this generation include Spike Lee, Oprah Winfrey, Sylvester Stallone, Connie Chung, and Bill Clinton. Boomers have earned a reputation for being rebellious, affluent, and independent. Most are in their thirties and forties. They have lived during a strong economy, they vividly remember the war in Vietnam, and they can't imagine the world without T.V.

The Builder Wave

The Builder wave came just before the Boomers. A get-it- done generation, Builders comprise two main groups: the G.I. Generation and the Silent Generation. Influential members of this group include Bob Hope, John Kennedy, Ronald Reagan, and Billy Graham. Builders tend to be loyal, faithful, and committed. Most are in their fifties or older and remember the Depression, World War II, and days with no T.V.

The Buster Wave

The generation that follows the Boomers is the Busters. They divide into two main subgroups: the Bust and the Boomlet. Influential members include Johnny Depp, Winona Ryder, Whitney Houston, Michael Jordan, and Greg Maddux. This may be the most abused, forgotten, and alienated generation of the three. The term *Buster* refers to people born between 1965 and 1983. This is our current generation of young people. Most are in their teens and twenties. They have experienced a fluctuating economy, Desert Storm, and MTV.

Changing Generational Waves

Anyone observing our culture today can easily see that drastic changes have been taking place, signaling that the influence of one generation is waning and that of younger generations is growing.

The Political Signal

Beginning with the 1988 presidential campaign, Americans have focused on generational changes. George Bush highlighted the coming generational change as a relay runner getting prepared to hand off the baton to the next generation. The *New York Times* highlighted this changing generational scene with its major headline for Wednesday, August 17, 1988: "BUSH CHOOSES SENATOR QUAYLE OF INDIANA, A 41-YEAR-OLD CONSERVATIVE, FOR NO. 2 SPOT." Subheadings to that lead article included "Emphasis on Youth" and "Baby Boomer with Right Credentials." Quayle, who was born February 4, 1947, became the first Baby Boomer to be on a national ticket. This was a highly visible signal that the torch was being passed to the younger generation and marked the start of a journey into the future.

If the choice of Dan Quayle as George Bush's running mate in 1988 highlighted the journey up the mountain, then the election of Clinton and Gore clearly pushed the Boomer Generation over the top. Newspaper headlines expressing the generational change taking place during the 1992 presidential election read, "NATION POISED TO ELECT NEW GENERATION" and "TIME OF LEADERSHIP COMES TO 'BABY BOOMERS.'"

Bill Nichols, writing in *USA Today*'s weekend edition of July 10–12, 1992, noted ". . . in Clinton's selection Thursday of the Tennessee senator as his running mate, a torch has been passed. For the first time, a presidential ticket has two candidates born after World War II—children of Vietnam instead of Vichy, the Temptations rather than Tommy Dorsey, and *All in the Family* not *Ozzie and Harriet.*"[2]

Quoted in the same article, Gore said, "Throughout American history each generation has passed on leadership to the next. That time has come again." When Bill Clinton moved into the White House, he was twenty-two years younger than his predecessor, George Bush. Only John F. Kennedy entered the presidency with a larger generation gap. He was twenty-seven years younger than outgoing President Dwight D. Eisenhower.

The T.V. Signal

Perhaps more than anywhere else, generational change in our society is evident in the television we watch. The majority of programs are geared to the eighteen to thirty-four-year-olds—the older Busters and younger Boomers. During the years when many Boomers were reaching their thirties, television programs began to include more sex, offensive language, and controversial societal issues than ever allowed before.

Changes occurring in network broadcasting mirror the changes in our society, as producers attempt to reach the largest possible audience.

For example, five years ago forty-one-year-old Jay Leno took over the *Tonight Show* from Johnny Carson, who was retiring at age sixty-five after thirty years as the show's host. The selection of Leno was an attempt to hold on to a portion of Carson's Builder audience but also designed to attract the Boomers and Busters.

More recently, *Star Trek* fans saw the theme of generational change reflected in the T.V. series *Star Trek: The Next Generation.* It was sort of a passing of the generational baton from Captain Kirk to Captain Picard.

The Religious Signal

Depending on whose research study you read, the typical church in the United States still has an average of only seventy-five to one hundred people attending worship each Sunday morning.[3] Yet, approximately every three weeks another church enters the league of a "megachurch."

To be a megachurch, a church must have a minimum of 2,000 members. In 1970 there were only ten such churches. Today, 300 megachurches with a combined membership of over 1 million people operate in the United States.[4]

In part, the megachurch boom is due to the baby boom. Older Baby Boomers who shied away from church for years are now turning to religion in fairly large numbers. The fortysomething Boomers are searching for personal meaning, religious education for their children, and answers to age-old questions.

This midlife generation (as well as their Buster children) often looks for a less traditional and ritualistic church with a contemporary message, music, and ministry. The decline of denominations, the growth of private Christian schools, the birth of specialized ministries such as MOPS (Mothers of Preschoolers), and the debut of celebrative worship services featuring contemporary music are all signals of generational change.

Similar to the political shift described before, there is a wave of generational change taking place among church, denominational, and parachurch leadership. An example is that of Pastor Greg Laurie and the Harvest Christian Fellowship of Riverside, California. Twenty-three years ago, a young nineteen-year-old Laurie started a Bible study with thirty people. Today forty-two-year-old Laurie's Harvest Church is the eighth largest church in the United States with about 9,000 members. Laurie has become one of our nation's new religious leaders through his annual Harvest Crusade. Since 1990 more than 750,000 people have attended this contemporary version of a Billy Graham crusade. In place of a large mass choir singing "Just As I Am," the audience at a Harvest Crusade hears Christian bluegrass, pop, and rock songs belted out by a band that includes singers, a drummer, and guitarists.

Serving the Generations

Clearly there is a new generational wave hitting the shore in the United States. No doubt additional illustrations of this fact could be added, but the three mentioned picture the changes quite nicely.

Why, though, should these changes concern us in the church? Our God is a changeless God as evident in such Scriptures as "For I, the LORD, do not change" (Mal. 3:6) and "Jesus Christ is the same yesterday and today, yes and forever" (Heb. 13:8). Yet, while we affirm that God is changeless and his truth unchangeable, we also recognize that generations change and Scripture records that it normally takes new leadership to communicate to new generations. Perhaps the best example in the Bible is that of Moses and Joshua. God selected Moses to lead the children of Israel out of the land of Egypt, but he used Joshua, not Moses, to reach a new generation in a new land.

Failure to understand and respond to the changing generational influences in the United States may have negative impact on our churches and ministry. Here are five of the several possible results.

1. A slow decline for many local churches and related denominations. The membership of churches that are unable to understand the changing generational dynamics appears to be on the decline. For example, the United Presbyterian Church lost nearly 1 million members between 1965 and 1985. During that decline someone described the "typical Presbyterian" as a "woman 48 years of age, white, and married."[5] Obviously this description was not a reflection of the emerging Boomer wave in the United States during those years. The Presbyterian Church (USA) has, of course, taken steps to try to reverse that trend. But the fact remains that many churches and denominations continue to lack understanding of the changing generational waves and are suffering decline due to an inability to reach the younger generations.

2. Fewer recruits for missions with a resulting loss of influence on unreached peoples. Immediately following World War II missionaries were recruited and sent to foreign fields in large numbers. Most were in their twenties and thirties and today are retiring and returning home. This changing of the guard is forcing missionary organizations to face the future. An illustration of this fact is the conference "Confronting Changing Patterns in Missions" conducted by the Advancing Churches in Missions Commitment (ACMC) in 1993.[6] The conference addressed the need to involve Baby Boomers in the cause of worldwide missions. It is apparent that most Boomers are not attracted to serve as career missionaries nor do they financially support foreign missions as their parents did. While the exact methodologies mission agencies will use in the future are not yet developed, clearly they must be designed to attract and meet the needs of people of younger generations.

3. *Less money with which to finance missions or other local church ministries.* The "Fund-Raising Institute Monthly Portfolio" reports that people between the ages of thirty-five and forty-nine make appreciably more financial gifts to nonprofit groups than any other age group.[7] This thirty-five to forty-nine age group is part of the Boomer Generation. If churches don't make an effort to understand what motivates giving in the younger generations, it will certainly result in a loss of financial support for our churches. Apparently younger people aren't as motivated by duty as the Builders are. They must believe in the cause they contribute to.

4. *A continual trend toward the liberal agenda in the United States.* While the younger generations appear to be returning to a more traditional lifestyle, they will likely support many liberal social issues such as gay rights, abortion-on-demand, and the ultra separation of church and state. If we hope to command any Christian authority in the boardrooms of our government, schools, and businesses through the year 2050, it is vital that we reach a significant number of people in the new generational waves, people who will be the decision makers for our country for the next sixty years.

5. *An inability to fulfill our God-given purpose to "make disciples of all the nations"* (Matt. 28:19). Since World War II more than 148 million people have been born in the United States. These are people for whom Christ died. If we estimate that 40 percent of them attend church on a given Sunday morning, some 88.8 million are candidates for new life in Christ. It is essential that we learn how to relate to these people so that we will be better prepared to follow in Jesus' steps to seek and save the lost (Luke 19:10).

Acts 13:36 is our example to follow. "For David, after he had *served the purpose of God in his own generation,* fell asleep, and was laid among his fathers, and underwent decay" (italics mine). The two phrases "served the purpose of God" and "in his own generation" clarify God's directions for ministry in a time of generational change.

The Purpose of God	Our Generation
Eternal	Temporal
Foundational	Cultural
Unchanging	Changeable

David understood his call to serve God's unchanging purpose among a particular generation in a changing generational scene. Ultimately, the reason we must seek to understand the changing generational waves is related to God's call and command to us as believers. *We are to serve his eternal and timeless purpose in a timely manner among a temporal generation.*

Surviving the Riptides of Change

I am fascinated with oceans. I grew up in Colorado and never saw an ocean until I visited California as a tourist when I was nineteen years old. I can still remember that cold March day when I first looked on the seemingly never ending expanse of the Pacific Ocean and went for a swim. It had been raining in California for about two weeks, and the water was rough and extremely cold. After swimming for about thirty minutes, I noticed that my knee was so stiff from the cold that I couldn't bend it at all. I came back on shore and as I was attempting to get warm a native Californian walked by and said, "You must be a tourist." I responded that I was and asked how he knew. He replied that only tourists went in the Pacific Ocean in March when it is bitter cold and the riptides so treacherous. I knew what he meant by cold (it took almost an hour before I could bend my knee completely), but I'd never heard of riptides.

Riptides, I have discovered, result when the return flow of waves moves away from the shore. The resulting undercurrent can pull with great force back out to the ocean whatever it catches. The larger the wave, the stronger the riptide will be.

Generational waves can collide in a kind of riptide. As the 76-million-member Boomer wave converges with the Builder wave and crashes into the Buster wave, numerous problems emerge.

Not only are these generational waves creating turbulence in our society, they are also causing turbulence in our churches. That's why it is essential to understand each generational wave and how it affects the other waves to effectively serve God's purpose today. Most of us are faced with the problem of ministering to a church that includes members of all three generational waves. We must try to understand the generations as well as how they affect each other.

Part 1

The Builder Wave

1

What Shaped the Builders?

Most of us have never heard of Dorothy Anderson Tormoehlen. She was hardly known outside her small Indiana community. Yet, at one time her image was one of the most familiar in the United States. She was the Morton Salt Girl.

There were actually several Morton Salt girls over the years, but Dorothy was the one with the pretty yellow dress and the ribbon in her hair found on containers in the 1920s and 1930s. As a niece of professional artist Mary Anderson, Dorothy was used regularly as a model for various renderings of children.

The Morton Salt Company began using a girl with an umbrella on their round, blue salt containers in 1914. Today, eighty-one years later, the phrase "when it rains, it pours" continues to remind us of the philosophy of a generation that felt if you got one problem, you were going to get even more.

Three Groups

For the purposes of this book we'll say the Builder Generation is made up of people who were born prior to 1946 and includes some 75 million people. Various names have been coined to describe the Builders. Some describe them today: Suppies (senior, urban professionals), Opals (older people with active lifestyles), Rappies (retired, affluent professionals), Whoopies (well-heeled older people), and Grumpies (grown-up mature people).

Perhaps the most characteristic names are Strivers, Survivors, and Builders.[1] Whether as adults or children, Builders strived through World War I and World War II. They survived Black Tuesday, the Great Depression, and Pearl Harbor. Through tough times and with hard work they built families, traditions, values, homes, friendships, communities, churches, and the greatest nation in the world.

We can divide the Builders into three smaller groups: the G.I. Generation, the Silent Generation, and the War Babies.

The G.I. Generation

The oldest Builders can be called the G.I. Generation because they came of age and fought during World War I and World War II. Born prior to 1925, they are today over seventy years old. There are in 1995 approximately 30 million people in the United States aged seventy and over representing 12 percent of the population. Seven presidents came from this G.I. Generation. President George Bush was the last.

Some Famous G.I. Generation Builders Who Are Still Influential Today

Steve Allen, 74
Lloyd Bentsen, 74
Tom Bradley, 78
Barbara Bush, 70

George Bush, 71
Johnny Carson, 70
Jimmy Carter, 71
Betty Ford, 77
Billy Graham, 77
Lena Horne, 78
Lady Bird Johnson, 83
Norman Mailer, 72
Paul Newman, 70
Ronald Reagan, 84
Oral Roberts, 77
Andy Rooney, 75
J. D. Salinger, 76
Mike Wallace, 77

Ages as of 1995

The Silent Generation

The Silent Generation is comprised of people born between 1926 and 1939 who in 1995 are between fifty-six and sixty-nine years old. There are currently around 30 million people in the United States in this age group. They are called the Silent Generation because when they were in their prime, in the fifties, they were fairly content and silent, especially when compared to the G.I. Generation. As a generation, they reached young adulthood during our country's years of prosperity in the 1950s. There was no need to be outspoken.

Some Influential Silent Generation Builders

Alan Alda, 59
Mel Brooks, 69
Rosalyn Carter, 68
Jerry Falwell, 62
James Earl Jones, 64
Quincy Jones, 62
Walter Mondale, 67
Colin Powell, 58
Della Reese, 63
Charles Robb, 56
Pat Robertson, 65
John Sununu, 56
John Updike, 63

Ages as of 1995

The War Babies

People born between 1940 and 1945 were called War Babies. They represent about 6 percent of our total population. Today they are between the ages of fifty and fifty-five years old.

Some Influential War Baby Builders

Joan Baez, 54
Ed Bradley, 54
Dick Cheney, 54
Angela Davis, 51
Neil Diamond, 54
Aretha Franklin, 53
Jesse Jackson, 54
Ted Koppel, 55
George Lucas, 51
Paul McCartney, 53
Geraldo Rivera, 52
Diana Ross, 51
Diane Sawyer, 50
Barbra Streisand, 53
Tammy Wynette, 53

Ages as of 1995

Formative Experiences

Looked at as a whole, these Builder subgroups reflect common values and perceptions, which probably developed from the slower pace of life experienced in their formative years. Generally speaking, the slower the pace of change, the more succeeding generations are alike. Since the pace of change was not as rapid in the first half of the twentieth century as it has been in the second half, these subgroups tend to share many characteristics.

As a generation moves through time and its members experience similar events, the members often begin to think, act, and feel in much the same way as other members of the generation.[2] What is taught and "caught" from parents, teachers, peers, and society contribute to the process. From early childhood each generation sees and interprets life events and experiences from within the context of the group. Over a period of time a particular generation becomes oriented to a particular way of thinking and perceiving. This process is called socialization.

The process of socialization begins at birth and continues into adulthood. A person's basic personality is formed by age four or five, but many of our preferences are actually determined during our late childhood and teenage years. The events that seem to have the most impact on people occur when they are between the ages of thirteen and twenty-two. The emotional responses to these events often stay with people for a lifetime, typically affecting two-thirds to three-fourths of people in a particular generation.

The good old days were different times for the various age groups within the Builders and very different from what Boomers and Busters have experienced. For many it was a time when families met around the dinner table. Mom cooked. There was no pizza or McDonald's. Items were purchased for their value, not because they were trendy. People fixed things that were broken. They believed in God, country, and family. Most people were loyal, faithful, and dependable, and they were survivors.

Many significant events occurred during the formative years of the Builder wave. The ones that follow seem to have been the most influential for most of the generation.

World War I

While only the very oldest of the Builders personally remember World War I, it is the beginning event of this generational wave. The Builders have fought in and supported more wars than any other generation in American history. World War I (1914–1918), often called the Great War and the war to end all wars, was the first truly global conflict. The United States tried to remain neutral, but with the sinking of the Lusitania (1915) and the beginning of unrestricted submarine warfare by Germany, the United States entered the war in 1917. World War I is remembered for its four long years of trench warfare and the use of poisonous gas resulting in an estimated 8 million troops killed. Hostilities were officially ended with the signing of the Treaty of Versailles. As American troops returned home, a new feeling of pride and hope resulted in a period of economic prosperity. The United States had been on the winning side of a global conflict, and everyone believed there would be no more wars.

The Roaring Twenties

The end of World War I ushered in a period of escapism called the Roaring Twenties (1921–1929). It was a time of prosperity when many Americans enjoyed a rise in the standard of living fueled in part by overspeculation in the stock market and easy credit. The entertainment industry flourished as crowds flocked to theaters and sports stadiums. During prohibition (1919–1933), many Americans broke the law by making liquor at home, and organized crime grew as gangsters bootlegged liquor. When investors overspeculated by purchasing stocks with money they did not have in hopes of reaping huge profits, stocks plunged, forcing individuals into bankruptcy and banks and businesses to fold. Massive agricultural, industrial, and financial problems led to the stock market crash of 1929, which took the roar out of the twenties.

The Great Depression

The stock market crash in 1929 was the beginning of the Great Depression, which continued through the 1930s. At the same time, dust storms resulting from drought and unwise farming methods caused severe damage, especially to farms in parts of Kansas, Nebraska, Texas, Oklahoma, and New Mexico. John Steinbeck's classic novel *The Grapes of Wrath* (1939) depicted the "Okies'" migration to California from the dust bowl of Oklahoma. More than 15 million people were unemployed during the height of the Depression. Thousands lost their homes, mortgages on farms were foreclosed, and millions lost their personal savings.

The majority of the Builders living today personally recall the Depression Era or have heard enough stories from their parents and grandparents to vicariously feel its effects. It is one of the primary socializing experiences of this generational wave and its impact cannot be overestimated.

Rural Lifestyle

The industrial age began pushing its way into the world of work about 1860, gradually beginning the process of making the Western world a powerful center of production. The rural lifestyle continued to play a major role in the socialization of the Builder Generation, however, until about 1950. In 1900, 37 percent of the labor force was involved in agricultural labor, and this percentage slowly declined to 12 percent in 1950.

The farmer's main objective had to be survival. It took hard work, dedication, and prayer to overcome the natural ups and downs of nature, but there was a predictability to life, with the regular planting and harvesting cycles. The small town atmosphere and slow pace allowed people to know, protect, and care for each other. Churches, schools, and family provided the necessary centers of social life.

The Automobile

Transportation was revolutionized during the lifetime of early Builders as they grew up with the development of the automobile. Henry Ford (1863–1947) built his first car in 1896 and formed the Ford Motor Company in 1903. He pioneered mass production techniques, using an assembly line and standardized parts. This system was able to mass produce the Model T and dramatically lower the price of cars. To entice his own workers to purchase his product, he started paying workers five dollars a day. By 1929 his company had become one of the largest manufacturers of cars in the world.

A love affair with the automobile began during the Builder Generation. Cars were simple and could be repaired by the average individual in his own driveway. But more importantly the automobile provided a new form of expression for personal freedom and individualism on which Americans place a high value. Many youth learned to drive cars before age twelve, and no respectable boy, having reached the legal driving age, would fail to get his driver's license.

Radio

In the 1930s, radio was new and began to capture the attention of the general public. For many Builder families radio was the main source of entertainment, and they became personal friends, if only over the air, with the likes of Edgar Bergen and Charlie McCarthy, Milton "Uncle Miltie" Berle, Eddie Cantor, Bud Abbott and Lou Costello, Fanny "Baby Snooks" Brice, and Bob Hope.

When Japan attacked Pearl Harbor and millions of young Americans were drafted, it meant giving up their favorite radio programs. Some became depressed because of it. By 1939 young recruits "were as addicted to radio as they are to television today."[3]

The military met the challenge by establishing the G.I. Network, eventually the Armed Forces Radio and Television Service, to provide news, music, sports, comedians, and girls. One of the most popular shows was *Command Performance,* featuring stars requested by the G.I.s. The first show on March 8, 1942, featured Eddie Cantor, Dinah Shore, Danny Kaye, Merle Oberon, and a rerun of the Joe Louis–Buddy Baer heavyweight fight.

The New Deal

At the Democratic National Convention of 1932, Franklin D. Roosevelt accepted his party's presidential nomination by declaring, "I pledge . . . myself to a new deal for the American people." Eventually his New Deal became an umbrella term for a wide range of relief programs adopted to stimulate economic recovery from the Great Depression of the 1930s.

Many Builders remember the beginnings of organizations and programs such as the Securities and Exchange Commission (SEC), the Federal Deposit Insurance Corporation (FDIC), the Civilian Conservation Corps (CCC), the Civil Works Administration (CWA), and the Federal Emergency Relief Administration (FERA).

Although these organizations and programs did not actually end the Great Depression they did provide much needed relief for many people and, most importantly, communicated government's commitment to deal with America's economic woes.

Big Bands

During the big band era of the 1930s many dance bands became popular, such as the Dorsey Brothers Orchestra. Jimmy and Tommy Dorsey formed their band in 1934. Some of their popular songs are "Amapola," "So Rare," "Marie," and "I'll Never Smile Again." Frank Sinatra achieved stardom with Tommy Dorsey's band and had a mass following of teenagers in the 1940s that remained unequaled until the Beatles became popular in the 1960s.

Benny Goodman, a clarinetist and bandleader, became known as the "king of swing." The Glenn Miller Orchestra played such songs as "Moonlight Serenade," "Tuxedo Junction," and "Chattanooga Choo Choo." Highly popular during the big band swing era, Glenn Miller dissolved his band in 1942 to lead the U.S. Army Air Force band in Europe and disappeared on a flight from England to Paris in 1944.

Other influential musicians included Louis "Satchmo" Armstrong, a jazz trumpet player and singer who originated scat, a type of improvised singing of meaningless syllables. He led a big band during the 1930s and 1940s and performed in films. William "Count" Basie formed his band in 1935 and performed in nightclubs, hotels, and theaters. His "One O'Clock Jump" is a jazz classic.

Other music styles helped to form Builder preferences. George Gershwin composed the popular concert piece *Rhapsody in Blue* (1924), musical comedies like *Funny Face* (1927) and *Of Thee I Sing* (1931), and the opera *Porgy and Bess* (1935).

Bing Crosby gained popularity through radio in the 1930s, entertained G.I.s during World War II, and eventually sold more than 30 million records, including the classic "White Christmas."

Pearl Harbor and World War II

On December 7, 1941, Pearl Harbor was the target of a surprise attack by the Japanese. Casualties included 18 ships sunk or damaged, 200 planes destroyed, and 2,323 servicemen killed. The attack spurred Congress to declare war on Japan, bringing the United States into World War II on December 8, 1941. Ask older Builders where they were when they heard that Pearl Harbor had been bombed, and most will be able to give you the exact place and time, so powerful was the impact of this event on the people of this generation.

The positive effect of Pearl Harbor was that it mobilized public opinion against the aggression of the Japanese and the Axis powers. World War II (1939–1945) once again brought an isolationist United States into a global conflict. The Builder wave pulled together as everyone did his or her part to win the war. Congress extended the draft to all men between twenty and forty-four years old. Men volunteered and were drafted into military service, women entered the workforce in record numbers, and those at home prayed and purchased war bonds in support of the war effort.

World War II created many heroes such as Gen. Dwight D. Eisenhower, Gen. Omar Bradley, Gen. Douglas MacArthur, Gen. George S. Patton, and Gen. George C. Marshall. Names like Midway, Iwo Jima, Corregidor, and Normandy bring back floods of memories to many Builders. The Normandy Invasion began on D day, June 6, 1944, and on May 1, 1945, Germany accepted unconditional surrender.

Harry S. Truman had become president following the death of Franklin D. Roosevelt, and on August 6, 1945, he ordered the atomic bomb dropped on Hiroshima and three days later on Nagasaki. Japan surrendered on August 15, 1945. The war ended, and our troops came home as victors from a war we believed we were destined to win. As some said, "God was on our side."

Rationing

During World War II rationing was used for the equitable distribution of scarce goods, and price controls helped limit inflation. There were twenty officially rationed items, including gasoline, sugar, meat, shoes, and tires. The Office of Price Administration issued stamps for commodities such as gasoline. Motorists were assigned window stickers with a priority ranking from A to E. Those who drove primarily for pleasure were issued an "A" sticker and could buy only two to five gallons of gas per week. Those with an "E" sticker—farmers, policemen, physicians, and drivers of emergency vehicles—could buy all the gas they wanted.

Stamps were issued for other rationed items. The number of stamps received depended on the number of people in the family. Some people gave or traded stamps to each other as needed, and all stamps had to be used by expiration dates to prevent hoarding. Early in the war, silk was diverted from the consumer industry to the war industry for the making of parachutes. When the silk supply from Japan was cut off, it was replaced by nylon. Women learned to mend their silk stockings, and nylon stockings became prized possessions.

The Korean War

During 1950–1953 the United States fought in the Korean War. This was the beginning of a new policy for containing Communism. For many Builders fear of Communism escalated at this time and would prevail during the next couple of decades. After the Korean War reached a stalemate, an armistice was signed on July 27, 1953, with the thirty-eighth parallel becoming the border between North and South Korea.

Family, School, and Church

Builders remember a time when life was centered around the three big influences of life: family, school, and church. The process of becoming an adult was carefully supervised by these three institutions. Social activities revolved around church and school activities. Family, school, and church most often worked together to build a fairly stable life, which helped people face difficult times and created a sense of unity. Couples rarely divorced. Fewer diversions meant that husbands and wives had more time for each other. Few women worked outside the home, so divorce, even in an unhappy marriage, was usually not an option for women. Traditional values permeated the home, community, and nation. Couples spent more time in childbearing and child rearing with fewer years to experience the "empty nest" or retirement.

Belief in God is taken for granted by most Builders, though to many religion means no more than that. To them we are "one nation under God," which means we do our duty to God and our country. Many remember a day of public school opening with the Pledge of Allegiance and the Lord's Prayer.

Characteristics

Win Arn, writing about this generation in *Live Long and Love It,* says, "We were here before panty hose, drip-dry clothes, ice makers, dishwashers, clothes dryers, freezers, and electric blankets"[4]; Builders were also born before the pill, television, penicillin, polio shots, Frisbees, hula hoops, frozen foods, Dacron, Xerox, the Kinsey Report, radar, credit cards, ballpoint pens, tape decks, CDs, electric typewriters, and computers.

There is a danger in characterizing an entire generation with the broad brush strokes that follow. Of course, many people in a generation will not fit into such a description, but when the generation is taken as a whole it seems to exhibit these characteristics.

Hard Workers

As a group Builders are hard workers. A rural lifestyle made this a necessity. Even with the emergence of the industrial age and the growth of factories and industry, hard work was required to survive in poor economic times. Labor laws were not strictly enforced, unions were just beginning to gain power, and working hard was the best way to keep your job and feed your family. Builders moved ahead due to diligence and perseverance.

Builders who have retired often continue to work hard. Common statements from Builders are, "I've got too many things to do" or "I'm busier in retirement than I was while working."

Savers

Fifty-four years ago Americans were learning to live with rationing and shortages in an effort to support the needs of World War II. It was a time of unity as everyone pitched in to support the Allied war effort. People got along. They adapted and learned to make something out of nothing. They found a way.

The Great Depression and the rationing of World War II taught Builders to save anything that might have value. You never knew when you might need that piece of string, used bar of soap, or piece of metal. The loss of money in the stock market crash and the bank closures created a desire to save money rather than spend it. Parents tried to save money in order to leave an estate to their children. A top priority was the future welfare of children.

Frugal

Luxuries were not available to most Builders until after the children left home, if then. During the lean years of the Depression adults and children learned frugality. Christmas mornings found stockings filled with nuts, apples, or oranges. Things were mended and repaired rather than thrown away—cardboard often stretched the life of shoes. Lights were turned out, heat was turned down, and energy-burning items were turned off to save money. In those days Builders used public transportation or walked to nearby stores. They planted gardens and canned food. Charging purchases on credit was not widely practiced. "Use it up; thin it out; make it last; do without" and "Make do or do without" were common sayings. Today in their fifties to nineties, Builders still tend to be frugal.

Patriotic

Many Builders fought in at least one war and are very patriotic. During the world wars the personal sacrifice required by all those who remained at home also created strong patriotic feelings. Holidays are important, particularly those having to do with patriotic themes such as Veterans Day, Independence Day, and Memorial Day. Builders, especially the older ones, love and zealously support their country, its leaders, and its ideals. This meant that Builders in general found it difficult to be sympathetic with Baby Boomers who fled the country to avoid the draft during the Vietnam War or burned draft cards and flags in the streets.

Loyal

Commitment is highly valued by Builders. They united together to win the greatest wars ever experienced. They worked together as families to make it through the Great Depression. They still debate theological issues and defend their religion. They "buy American." Builders often work for only one company for a lifetime, often on the same job. They trust the company, union, or government to take care of them for a lifetime.

Builders often see things as black and white rather than in grays. They do things because they believe it is right to do them.

Private

"We don't air our dirty laundry in public" was a regular admonishment from Builder parents to their Boomer children. "Good company, good food, good night!" was another saying that stressed the need for privacy.

Builders like the idea of knowing about people but resist sharing deep concerns that would allow them to really know each other. Small groups for Bible study are fine but not for personal sharing of deep hurts or needs. Such sharing is only acceptable within the family. Topics of a personal or intimate nature are taboo. Personal expressions of a sexual nature even between husbands and wives are not for public display. As they grew up many Builders never received a hug or experienced closeness with their fathers.

Cautious

The times of simply surviving taught older Builders to settle for modest goals, hold on to savings, and be thankful for simply having a job. Few people were protected by life insurance, and the Depression stopped many from saving for retirement. Their lives were lived at the mercy of an unplanned economy and limited occupational opportunities. Luxuries had to wait until after the children left home, and even then, many Builders were too cautious to indulge.

Respectful

During their formative years most Builders were taught to have respect for people. Children were taught to respect their parents and elders. Workers respected their bosses. Privates in the military respected their officers. The position was respected even if the individual in the position was not.

As a result, Builders tend to be more thoughtful, considerate, and kind to others than the succeeding generations. Theirs was not a "me" generation as much as a "we" generation. They go out of their way to help neighbors and support each other in times of need.

Dependable

Builders see value in self-discipline, sticking together, and staying with the task in the face of any adversity. "If the job is worth doing, it's worth doing well," is their motto. Builders have continued to work hard even as the times have become more affluent.

Stable

For Builders who grew up in a rural lifestyle, life was fairly predictable. You rose early to do the chores. You cultivated, planted, watered, cultivated some more, and waited for the harvest, which eventually came. You planted and harvested at about the same times every year.

Certainly life was unpredictable in terms of the Depression and war, but in the things closer to home, such as family, work, and church, things were the same. As the times have changed and life has become more unpredictable, Builders try to remain stable, holding to the same goals and ideals their generation has valued for years.

Intolerant

As a group Builders tend to be less tolerant than the Boomers or Busters of people who are different from them. This is partly due to the fact that most Builders have spent most of their lives in fairly homogeneous communities. They have resisted change, believing the way they and their parents have done things is the best way.

Conclusion

For Builders, hard work, self-discipline, and sacrifice have paid off. They survived the difficult years of war and economic depression and believe that the affluence of the 1950s and 1960s proved that striving and surviving were the right way to go.

Today in the United States, 31 million Builders are sixty-five years old or older. Most are retired, but many are still involved in some type of employment or volunteer work. Because Builders tend to be thrifty, many have substantial savings that allow them to live in retirement quite comfortably. Retirement plans and social security also help provide financial security. These Builders tend to travel extensively, enjoying cruises and tours with others their age. Some live part of the year in the northern United States and move south during the cold winter months.

Even though our bodies become less durable with age, because of medical advances and good health care, many older Builders enjoy good health. There are, of course, others who suffer from chronic illness, which may inhibit their ability to get around easily and care for themselves.

As we consider older Builders we must include those who do not have sufficient financial resources to live comfortably. Many of these senior citizens are forced to struggle daily to make their financial resources meet their basic needs. They fear losing their homes or needing expensive medical care.

Many have lost a spouse through death and suffer the shock and loneliness of being alone after many years of married life.

Builders between the ages of fifty and sixty-five are in various stages of transition. Some are experiencing the "empty-nest" syndrome. Some are beginning to think about retirement or are actually beginning retirement.

The financial concerns of these Builders may be major and different than they faced before—college for their children, nursing-home care for elderly parents, learning to live on a fixed income.

"When it rains, it pours" became a watchword for the Builder Generation. The Morton Salt Girl's prophecy was fulfilled in several dramatic ways that continue to fashion the older members of this generation.

Younger Builders, however, now are a powerful generation. The power of those fifty-plus-year-olds can be seen in the following statistics:

- Eighty percent of Americans over fifty are home owners.
- Those over fifty have 43 percent of all discretionary income.

- Seventy-five percent of the nation's wealth is in the hands of these fifty-plus-year-olds.
- Eighty percent of savings and loan deposits, plus virtually all of the stocks, are in their hands.[5]

While generational change is taking place, wise church leaders will continue to provide effective ministry to this powerful generation.

2

Builders and the Church

In his old age, John Quincy Adams illustrated that age is more part of the mind than of the body. One day while Mr. Adams was walking slowly down a Boston street, a friend stopped and asked him, "And how is John Quincy Adams today?" "Thank you," replied the former president. "John Quincy Adams is well, quite well, I thank you. But the house in which he lives at present is becoming quite dilapidated. It is tottering upon its foundations. Time and the seasons have nearly destroyed it. Its roof is pretty worn out. Its walls are much shattered, and it trembles with every wind. The old tenement is becoming almost uninhabitable, and I think John Quincy Adams will have to move out of it soon. But he himself is quite well, quite well."[1]

Some people use three categories to describe the Builder Generation: Go-goes, Slow-goes, or No-goes. Most, of course, are very much in the Go-go category and are able and willing to respond to a church's ministry. They continue to have ownership of many areas of church life, particularly in the smaller church. Even though many Builders are open to change, there are a significant number who will exercise their power as needed to keep things the same. Since Builder influence will continue to be felt in churches due to the networks of relationships and the informal influence exercised through them, it will be wise to understand what drives their ministry in the church.

This "Make-Do Generation" has found faith, encouragement, and support during difficult times in their churches. In the first half of this century, churches were often found at the center of a town's social life. It is no accident that the churches of that era were found at the center of town. Their location was a physical statement of a true reality.

Builders who grew up in the forties and fifties were trained to attend Sunday school and church, and for many of them this habit continues in the nineties. If Builders do not attend church because of a spiritual commitment, they may attend because of a social commitment. Most Builders believe in God, with the percentage of atheists and agnostics lower in this generation than in the other two.

While Boomers and Busters can be found in disproportionate numbers in larger churches, the Builders are most often found in small churches. Commitment to Christ means being a member of a church and supporting its activities, so the church has become central to their way of life. They believe that if they support the church's programs, the church will be successful, even if it is small.

Builders, then, have a strong sense of obligation to serve the church. They are often at the heart of their churches, in part due to their dedication and willingness to serve. They are the most church-going generation, and they give graciously to charities—especially religious organizations.

The church's answer to ministry needs until the early 1970s was programs. If we needed to reach the lost, we had a week of revival. If we needed to reach out to those in other countries, we started a missions program. To carry out the goals of programs, committees and boards had to be established. Churches established during those years were often organized around a number of committees and boards. People who showed particular interest in a special program were placed on a committee to oversee it. Thus the Sunday school had an education committee, the missions program had a missions committee, and the nursery had a nursery committee.

One of the main assumptions about ministry during the first half of the twentieth century concerned knowledge of the Bible. Most believed that if anyone knew enough of the Bible, they would do the right thing. Bible study focused almost exclusively on learning the content of the Bible—Scripture memory associations sprang up for adults, and Bible quizzes became quite popular for children and youth.

A great deal of time was given to Bible study and prayer, and Builders did learn much about the Bible, but there was not always a lot of time given to defining their personal belief system. Many learned the words of the Bible without letting them penetrate their lives. Today Builders have a continued interest in Bible study and are often the teachers of Bible study groups.

Ministry through Foreign Missions

Following World War II the driving force in financial stewardship for Builders was missions. Returning G.I.s had seen new regions of the world. They had seen the results of sin in the Holocaust and the great need for Christ in the countries of Europe and Asia. The burst of missions and mission agencies immediately following World War II was fueled by economic growth and the willingness of Builders to financially support foreign missions.

Still, today, missionary efforts are largely funded by Builders. This, of course, is to be lauded. Untold thousands, perhaps millions of people, have been brought into the kingdom of God through foreign missions. Yet, for many Builders, true ministry is defined as only missions. If ministry does not flow toward missions, it is of little use. Builders often say that a "Missions-giving church is a growing church," and that implies that a church's focus must be on worldwide missions. Though the result has been the growth of missions, it has often been at the expense of home-based ministry, which has sometimes meant a weakened home church. This eventually leads to less being given to foreign missions.

Today Builders sometimes feel a need to defend their view of ministry, and they are slow to adopt any new way of doing church ministry. Builders are usually satisfied with modest and plain church facilities. They may live, drive, and work in air conditioning, yet they resist putting air conditioning into their churches, feeling that such expenditures for the church building are too extravagant. Builders are hesitant to go into debt for church facilities or land purchases.

Many Builders have attended the same church for years. They have come to appreciate the songs, order of service, and decorations that have remained the same for a long time. Builders resist change in their churches because change destroys the stability and the security they expect. In making changes in a traditional church, care should be taken to affirm the validity of previous ministries, underscore the biblical basis of past ministries, present changes as an extension of the past, and move in a loving, accepting, and patient manner. As much as possible, when making changes in key ministry areas, there should be two ministries—one in the new format and one in the style appreciated by the Builders.

Loyalty to Denominations

Builders usually are strongly committed to their denomination or theological perspective. While Boomers and Busters change churches easily, Builders find it difficult to leave their church or denomination. They will support a church with problems or even a declining church, since they feel it would be disloyal to leave. Churches with strong denominational identities tend to hold on to their Builders even when they relocate. However, the same churches regularly lose many of their younger members to churches that offer greater choices or a more upbeat style of music.

For Builders, corporate worship is a time of quietness and contemplation of God. A worship service that requires minimal audience participation and that includes hymns, expository or content-oriented sermons, a pastoral prayer, recognition of guests, and organ/piano music is preferred.

Ministering to Builder Believers

Approximately 20 percent of church members today are Builders over the age of sixty-five. Few churches, however, have ministries targeted to this age group. For example, in a survey of 200 churches by Dr. Win Arn in 1989, fully one-fourth (26 percent) of the churches had no specific activities or programs for these Builders. The remaining three-fourths of the churches indicated only superficial ministries to their senior members, such as hospital visitation, food distribution, or provision of hearing aids in the worship services.[2]

Some older Builders have given up, feeling that they are not needed anymore. Others no longer serve in churches, believing that they have done their time and now the younger generations should take over.

The truth is that many people have done their greatest work in old age. For example, former President Ronald Reagan served as president of the United States while in his seventies. While in their eighties Albert Schweitzer oversaw a hospital in Africa, Michelangelo designed the Church of Santa Maria degli Angeli, Winston Churchill wrote his four-volume *A History of the English-Speaking Peoples,* and Benjamin Franklin worked out a compromise that led to the ratification of the U.S. Constitution. Grandma Moses painted her first picture at age seventy-six, Colonel Sanders made his first million when in his seventies, Amos Alonzo Stagg didn't retire from collegiate coaching until the age of eighty-three, and George Adamson of *Born Free* fame ran his primitive wildlife camp in eastern Kenya until his death at age eighty-three.[3]

There seems to be a tendency in some churches to ignore older Builders, but they need the ministry of the church. Many have faithfully served Christ and his church in difficult times and still have much to offer in personal wisdom and active ministry. They are due our honor and respect.

As we saw in the previous chapter, the personal needs of younger Builders may be very different from those of others within their group and from those of older Builders, but all Builders seem to have similar spiritual needs. Builders usually are not looking to their churches for entertainment, although they need and enjoy the socializing the church provides. Most Builders want to learn, grow, and serve in the church.

Aging may bring along physical difficulties, but for most aging is in the mind more than in the body. "Individuals can be elderly at age fifty, or they can be young at age ninety."[4] "The thermostat of true aging is set by one's mind, by serenity of spirit, by continued growth, and by purposeful activity."[5]

Satchel Paige, the legendary baseball player, once asked "How old would you be if you didn't know how old you are?"[6] His question points out the view of many gerontologists that old age is essentially a matter of the mind. Some Builders are recent retirees who are still full of energy. The fifty-five- to sixty-five-year-olds will probably want to be involved in many activities. However, the older retirees may prefer less ministry involvement. For them, service to the church will need to be done in shorter chunks of time. Many have worked hard all their lives and will want to take long vacations during their retirement. Their ministry will need to be planned around their times of travel.

Here are a few ideas on how to keep Builders involved in their churches.

Group Activities

Builders may find that their families and friends have moved far away and live in other cities. Their need for meaningful relationships continues, and churches can provide groups, classes, and activities to help develop new relationships and maintain old ones. Builders like being with other Builders. Group activities built around tasks and trips will be the best attended. Try monthly luncheons or bimonthly trips.

Sunday School

Sunday school was the main ministry when many Builders were in their prime, and they still see it as the primary ministry of the church. The maturity and wisdom of Builders can be used more wisely than we've often done in the past. Consider using Builders in panel discussions, teaching parenting classes, counseling young family members, leading Bible studies, and teaching new believers or new-members classes.

Missions Projects

Builders usually provide strong financial support to the church. Many have established consistent habits of giving to the church. Those who are enjoying financial security and who no longer have dependent children often give generously.

Their strong emotional tie to missions will continue, and churches should work with this by asking Builders to help support short-term missions trips for Busters. Of course, they ought to be encouraged to go on short-term missions trips themselves.

In-Depth Bible Study

Builders enjoy classes on books of the Bible, theology, and eschatology. They also benefit from such classes as those on handling finances during retirement, or restoring relationships with adult children, or effective grandparenting.

Groups and classes that have as their objective personal growth may not be as attractive as ones that stress the learning of content, but they may be what Builders need most. Many Builders have grown up believing they should be reserved about their feelings as well as their faith. They may need to learn how to reach out to others and share their faith.

Focus on Marriage and Grandparenting

Many Builders have had happy or at least enduring marriages. Family, home, and marriage have been a major part of their lives. Effective ministry to this generation must carry on this focus by covering new family needs based on the Builder's life stage. Unfortunately, divorce among Builders is becoming more prevalent than in the past. Ministry to recently divorced people and to those whose spouses have died is essential.

Focus may also need to change to grandparenting at this time. A grandparent may have a wide range of concerns from simply being a good baby-sitter to knowing what discipline is appropriate. Churches should help Builders be good grandparents by providing counsel, classes, and resources. Builders who have had successful experiences in any of these areas can be used in teaching others.

A throng of Builders are finding that the term "unplanned parenthood" has a whole new meaning. And for most, parenting the second time around is a lot more difficult than the first time. In 1990 the U.S. Census Bureau noted that more than 3 million children lived in households headed by grandparents. "Based on my experience, it's become an epidemic," says Syl DeToledano, a Long Beach, California, social worker who started a Grandparents as Parents support group in 1987. Since then she has helped start more than 130 groups across the United States.[7]

Grandparents become parents again for several reasons. Their child may be unemployed, in jail, or abusive. The fastest growing reason in the 1990s is alcohol and drug addiction among parents. When children are placed with grandparents because their parents have one or several of these problems, the children come with emotional, medical, and behavioral problems. This makes parenting the second time around difficult or next to impossible. The positive side is that the child's well-being is taken care of and, of course, you can't be old with a kid around. Grandparents in this situation, though, need the understanding and support the church can provide.

Contact with Other Generations

Builders should not relate in ministry only to other Builders. Effective programs have been built around the goal of intergenerational involvement. Even though relations between older Builders and Boomers were strained in the sixties, much of the animosity has dissipated, although some Builders still have not reconciled their differences with their Boomer children.

Builders often relate well to their grandchildren—the Busters. As we will see in chapters to come, the Busters are returning to values similar to those of their grandparents, and, as a result, strong bonds are developing between them and their Builder grandparents.

In ministry this means two things. Churches should seek to bring Busters and Builders together, and if there is tension between Builders and Boomers attempts should be made to encourage reconciliation. Churches can provide a great service to both generations by providing forums for discussion and reconciliation.

Retirement

Retirement means different things to different people. Some have said:

> Retirement is what follows your midlife crises.
> Retirement is twice as much husband and half as much money.
> Retirement comes just before senility.

A study by Dr. Don Anderson found that the thought of retirement evoked four major feelings—fantasy, fear, frustration, and fascination.[8] Some see retirement as fantasy. They cannot even imagine what it is going to be like to not have to go to work each morning. Others have great fears: fears relating to how they are going to live financially, selling a home, moving in with children or into a nursing home, or fear of death. Retirement is the last big phase of life through which we go before death. Some face retirement with a great deal of frustration. Perhaps there are goals they have never achieved, relationships that have not been healed, and missed opportunities they will never be able to retrieve. Some face retirement with anticipation of the possibilities before them—a part-time career in another field, time for a hobby, travel. In short, retirement is simply one phase of life. As such it leaves us with certain vulnerabilities, though it also offers many new opportunities.

Central Baptist Church in Jacksonville, Texas, has a ministry to Builders called "Live Long and Like It." Thirty-eight people serve on special committees to organize groups, such as Walk-a-Mile club, Snap, Crackle 'n' Pop (an exercise group), Bible studies, a library interest group, a handbell choir, a ceramics class, and a genealogical workshop. They have a "Volunteer Service Corps" to help older people meet the needs of and reach out to other seniors in the community.

First Baptist Church of San Angelo, Texas, has a Glory Choir of 113 senior adult members. As Dr. Arn says, "It is particularly true of seniors . . . that they do not seek or desire 'busy work.' . . . time is too precious. But meaningful kingdom work . . . yes."[9]

One of every three retirees returns to work.[10] Their reasons are varied: to earn money, for social contact, or to fill empty hours. Most do not return to a forty-hour-a-week job but prefer to work part-time. A growing body of evidence suggests that those who work part-time are more likely to stay healthy.

During the 1980s the number of retirees over the age of fifty-five who reentered the workforce more than doubled, and this is likely to continue. Life cannot be so neatly divided into stages of education, work, and retirement as once was the case. Builders want to work, even if it's just for something to do. However, according to figures cited in the February 1993 AARP bulletin, the number of Builders who couldn't find a job rose 18 percent. Once again, churches can provide ministry. They can provide information for businesses and Builders on job placement.

Personal Pastoral Care

The complex issues facing individuals today make pastoral care one of the more difficult areas of ministry. Today's pastor cannot be an expert in every new area of personal need. Builders can be trained in pastoral care. Their experience probably means they will be able to love and be willing to listen to others. Studies have found that older people find it much easier to say "I love you" than young people and thus may be the best ones to extend their love through pastoral care. Using Builders in this way will extend pastoral care to a larger percentage of the church body. When a pastor is not available, Builders can be.

Plan for the Future Church

Many Builders have faithfully served God in their churches, but it is often true that their children and grandchildren are not serving God and are not comfortable in the churches that Builders enjoy. We need to help Builders see that ministry must be formed and shaped with their children and grandchildren in mind. Builders can help build churches to which their grandchildren will want to come.

Conclusion

General Douglas MacArthur liked to read the following short statement about age. On his wall he kept the following words, "Youth is not a time of life, it is a state of mind. You are as young as your faith, as old as your fear, as young as your hope, as old as your despair."[11]

Builders will find the aging process less traumatic if they find meaningful and challenging ways of using their time. Churches can have a major role in helping Builders find places of service.

3

Elderly Builders

The writings of Allen G. Odell are legendary among Builders. He first began writing in 1925, and for almost four decades his short poems were seen and read at over 7,000 locations in forty-five states. In the mid-1960s a set of his poems was placed in the Smithsonian Institution. His favorite poem was:

Within this vale
Of toil and sin
Your head grows bald
But not your chin
. . . Burma Shave.

Allen's dad owned the Burma-Vita Company. In 1925 for 200 dollars he put up the first Burma Shave signs himself in southern Minnesota. By 1948 the popular signs were gradually disappearing, victims of high speed travel and interstate highways. The signs were discontinued in 1963 after the company was sold to the Philip Morris Company.

Allen Odell was an ad man's gem. He understood his audience and communicated to them in a way that will be remembered for years to come. His Builder audience needs to hear greater words than those Burma Shave poems. They have a need to hear the saving words of salvation. As Builders continue to age, their time to hear and receive Christ grows shorter with each passing day. Many are open to the gospel and will listen and believe if churches reach out to them in appropriate ways. Serving the needs of elderly Builders will develop openness and credibility for the sharing of the gospel at a later time.

Common Areas of Concern

Today's elderly Americans have never had so many options for their retirement years, and seniors are living longer to enjoy it! Only between 4 and 8 percent of American seniors are actually living in total care facilities. The great majority of Builders are living independent, active lives.

Aging does press its own set of unique needs into the lives of Builders, and churches can offer answers to spiritual concerns as well as help in other areas. Churches can help members through personal problems by responding in appropriate ways to their needs and by providing a wide range of participational options—personal, family, and social activities. Aging Builders will need the support of churches in the years ahead as they encounter some, if not all, of the following.

Financial Concerns

One of the myths surrounding elderly Americans is that they are all poor. Certainly some are well below the poverty line, but "between 1969 and 1986 the official poverty rate for the elderly declined from 25 percent to 12 percent."[1] That does not mean, however, that the elderly are not concerned about finances. A report in the *Gallup Poll Monthly* noted, "The leading concerns among older Americans are health and financial security. One-third of those fifty years and older expect their health to worsen by the year 2000 and nearly as many (29 percent) expect their financial situation to worsen."[2]

Many elderly Builders are living on fixed incomes. Whether it is social security or diminished income from investments, they have to struggle to live on their income, and many have had to live at a lower standard of living than they did when younger. There are elderly people, however, who have been able to amass large estates, and they struggle to know what to do with their unexpected wealth.

In past years, retirees usually had to rely on a good savings account for their living. Today retirement income comes from a variety of sources. Knowing how to manage these funds can be a challenge for individual retirees. Churches can reach out to them by offering financial planning help or putting them in touch with agencies that can help.

Churches can help older Builders learn how to recognize and avoid fraud. Unscrupulous people prey on the elderly with phony investment opportunities involving land sales, time shares, stocks and bonds, commodities and futures trading, gems, precious metals, franchises and distributorships, oil and gas, art, rare coins, and financial planning services. The church can provide workshops to educate the elderly. For information, contact your local Better Business Bureau.

Housing

Housing issues are often problems for the elderly. They may have property to sell and decisions to make about what housing is affordable for them. It may be that people on fixed incomes would benefit from banding together in shared housing arrangements. Housing may be a particular problem for single seniors, and in today's society, divorce and widowhood create a longer period of living alone than used to be the case. Churches can assist with these problems by providing written resources, counseling, and classes. They may be able to set up networking to inform their senior members of affordable housing or roommates.

Personal Safety

Personal safety is and will continue to be a major concern for elderly Builders. Some elderly people who live alone carry beepers, which can alert friends or neighbors that they have fallen or met with some mishap. The NRA offers a program on how to protect yourself without the use of firearms—the Refuse to Be a Victim course. Mainly for women, this three-hour seminar offers tips on home and personal security.

A church, too, can offer courses on personal safety and provide literature on the topic. Some churches may be able to train individuals to do safety checks on homes, giving ideas on how to make them safer.

Health

In 1950, the average life expectancy was 68.2 years. Today the average life expectancy is 72 years for men and 78 years for women. At the turn of the century, less than 1 million people in the population had reached their 75th birthday. As of 1990 more than 9 million people, over one-fourth of the older adult population, had turned 75 years old. By 2020 life expectancy will be 78.1 years. It is estimated that by 2040 life expectancy for males will be 87 years and 92 years for females.[3]

The Gallup study that was cited earlier showed that today's Builders worry about their future health. Many elderly Builders are already suffering from a variety of illnesses. Some studies have found that 85 percent of older Americans suffer from conditions that could be improved through better nutrition. Cited in the *Journal of the American*

Medical Association, one study showed that half of independent individuals sixty-five years of age or older have specific nutritional deficiencies.[4]

To maintain good health older Americans must have a nutritious diet and proper exercise. They should have regular medical checkups and have the resources to obtain needed medications and immunizations. When money is tight, however, food and medical care are often the areas where elderly Americans choose to scrimp.

Churches can help by providing their elderly members with hot meals or groceries, or they can help them find such services elsewhere. Transportation to clinics is a valuable service as well as exercise classes and workshops on nutrition. Church members with expertise could help the elderly understand and complete Medicare forms.

Adequate Transportation

It is a time of crisis in the life of an elderly Builder when he or she can no longer qualify for a driver's license. It is not only a loss of freedom to get around but an emotional loss as well because it puts one's competence into question. Without a driver's license an individual must rely on public transportation or family and friends. Public transportation is not always safe in larger cities, nor is it convenient. Many elderly people would prefer not to have to rely on family and friends for rides. Churches could provide regular transportation to grocery stores, malls, and clinics for the older Builders in their immediate community as a way to build relationships for greater ministry in the future.

Preparation for Death

No one likes to think about his or her own death. People approaching the end of their physical lives often go through denial and put off making important decisions until it is too late. Those who take the time to prepare for the end of life find that there are numerous benefits. When decisions are made concerning a will, a living trust, and burial preparations, the elderly person will have peace of mind that his wishes will be carried out at his death. It also benefits the surviving family members by reducing the number of decisions that must be made at an emotional time.

Since many elderly people don't know where to start in making these preparations, churches can help by offering classes or workshops on wills, avoiding probate, living trusts, funerals, and funeral preparations. Assisting elderly Builders with physical preparations for death leads naturally into a discussion about spiritual preparation. It may be a time to lead some to the Lord and to help Christian seniors face death with the assurance of eternal life.

Spiritual Needs

Often as people age, they begin to think seriously about spiritual matters. Builders were taught not to share personal concerns in public, and many have avoided discussing such issues, but they may yearn to do so. Common Builder wisdom advised one not to discuss religion or politics, so churches must proceed with caution. Providing forums that deal with broad spiritual topics such as salvation, death, forgiveness, and eternal existence would be a good first step. If these are presented in a respectful, loving manner, follow-up may be possible. This could be done by appointment in their homes, which would allow for further discussion on a personal level.

Leisure Time

Retired Builders may not have developed interesting and healthy ways to spend their time. Many Builders spend too much time alone and watching television. Boredom is a major problem. People who worked hard at a career may not have had the time or inclination to develop hobbies or other interests.

Churches can minister to their retired members by providing opportunities for them to get together during the week at Bible studies, exercise classes, trips to the library or museum, and the like. Older Builders should be encouraged to help where they are able in church ministries. They can be involved in Vacation Bible School, day-care programs, foster grandparents programs. They can tend the church library, plant flowers, do visitation.

Sometimes retired people feel they are not needed and have trouble seeing where they can fit into church ministry. With a little encouragement, many will find areas of meaningful service and good ways to spend their time.

Substance Addiction

Alcoholism is as common among older Americans as it is among the younger. Their addiction may go undetected since they do not have to go to work every day, do not usually commit crimes, and can stay at home for long periods. Builders do not talk about substance abuse, seeing it as a weakness to be ashamed of. They are, therefore, not likely to receive treatment. Loneliness often leads to drinking or other substance abuse. This is another reason why churches must provide activities that will help older Builders get out of the house and build new relationships. Some churches may even be able to provide in-depth counseling. All should be able to refer their members to Christian counselors.

Elder Abuse

Elder abuse is a growing crime in the United States. Not as well understood as child abuse, it is an issue that is likely to gain much more publicity in the future as the general population continues to age.

Dr. Susan Lichtman, director of the Center for Aging Resources, defines elder abuse as "any action against a senior using violence or threat of violence against the senior's will."[5] Elder abuse often occurs when an older Builder lives with his or her children or grandchildren. It also happens in nursing homes and other elder-care facilities. Churches must speak out against abuse of any type. Making counseling or just a listening ear available may be helpful to the abused and the abuser.

Reaching Unchurched Builders

The changing structure of the family has left many Builders with weak support networks. "Fifty years ago," says Dr. Lichtman, "many people were in each generation, with few generations alive at a given time, sort of a flattened triangle. People had more children. Now, the family looks more like a bean pole, with multiple generations alive at any given time with few numbers in each generation."[6]

This change in the family structure is creating a need for caregiving with fewer caregivers available. This is an open door of opportunity for churches that wish to reach the Builder Generation. Churches can meet the real needs of people who are hurting and at the same time reach this generation with the gospel of Jesus Christ. Here are some ideas.

Set Up a Hot Line

Consider offering a hot line service for people to call who need help. There are some national hot lines for Builders. By calling 1-800-955-7848, Builders can have answers to general health questions provided by the American Physical Therapy Association. Along with the practical advice, callers are sent a free brochure on "Fitness, A

Way of Life." (See the resources section of this book for other phone numbers.)

A creative church can offer a similar hot line that would try to help callers with problems and questions on a variety of subjects. A number of different brochures on the same topics could be provided free for the asking.

Provide Support Groups

Family ties are crucial in times of crisis. A study reported in January 1993 found that when things are going well for Builders, children are relatively unimportant. However, when a crisis hits, such as deteriorating health or loss of a spouse, support from children is crucial to prevent depression. About 35 percent of elderly parents receive some sort of help from their children in the form of shopping, transportation, and household chores. Nearly 60 percent receive emotional support such as simply having someone to talk to.[7] Builders who have this family support have better mental health than those who do not.

Between 40 and 65 percent of our elderly do not receive the support they need from their children. The community may provide help in some areas, but it's often the emotional support that is left wanting. A church can form small groups for the elderly in the neighborhood that will provide time for talking, offering each other advice, and socializing.

Government health statistics report that more than 60 million people are actively involved in caring for an ailing loved one. The AARP reports that more than 7 million households have an unpaid caregiver providing assistance on a daily basis to a family member age fifty or older.[8] Family members who care for elderly parents or grandparents need support. They need to know that someone else understands their frustrations. It is also helpful to know there is someone to call when they need a respite. A support group can meet these needs, providing a forum for airing frustrations and stepping in with practical help when needed.

It is likely beyond the ability of most churches to provide long-term respite for caregivers. However, it may be possible to offer assistance to free caregivers briefly for short-term breaks so that they may go on errands, shop, or simply enjoy time for themselves. There may be teenagers who would be interested in visiting an elderly Builder or who could help with errands and small chores around the home. Offer assistance for housecleaning, companion care, and handyman service. For information on providing long-term respite, contact the Group Activities and Respite Program at Hunter College's Brookdale Center on Aging in New York City, 425 E. 25th St., New York, NY 10010-2590, (212) 481-7670.

Schedule Traditional Activities

An interesting study of widows over fifty conducted by Sara Staats, a professor at Ohio State University, found that widows were satisfied with their lives and as optimistic about the future as married women in the same age group. One way widows adjusted was by developing a network of friends and activities to keep them active and occupied. The older widows were the most involved in social activities.[9]

Consider providing some traditional holiday activities for Builders who may be without the family support normally associated with holidays. The smell of Christmas trees, cider, spices, or Thanksgiving dinners will fill the air with nostalgia and stimulate memories of the past. By offering a place for Builders to gather around the traditional holiday sounds, smells, and activities, your church can provide a ministry to those who might not otherwise hear the Good News of Christ and his love.

Help with Social Security and Income Taxes

With each new year there are changes having to do with social security that may be difficult to understand. Perhaps there are people in your church who worked in the social security field or Medicare agency who could make it their ministry to keep up with the changes and work with individuals who need assistance.

You may also be able to provide assistance to the elderly with filing their income tax returns.

Sponsor Trips

An increasing number of older Americans are traveling. Longer life spans, healthier living, and large financial estates are making it possible for Builders to take trips throughout the world. Whether as individuals or as part of a travel club, Builders are seizing opportunities to travel to places they've dreamed of visiting. Churches should consider using tourist trips as a means of ministry to unchurched Builders. Tourist trips could be scheduled with the express purpose of bringing Christian Builders and unchurched Builders together for one or two weeks. To work, at least 50 percent of the people on the tour must be unchurched. The Christian Builders who go on the trip should be very relational and be coached in how to develop friendships that will continue on after the trip is finished. After the trip, the unchurched members of the tour should be invited to other appropriate events that will expose them to the gospel.

Offer Classes

Most elderly Builders still like to learn. A clear example of this is the growing Elderhostel movement. Elderhostel, which began in 1975, has blossomed into an international educational program offered at more than 2,000 locations. In 1992, 250,000 Builders went to classes coast-to-coast and on field trips overseas. The minimum age is sixty, but spouses as young as fifty are allowed. Classes are offered on a wide variety of subjects from whittling to Civil War history.

There is no reason why churches cannot develop similar classes and activities as a means of building bridges to unchurched Builders. These classes can be taught by church members or by volunteers from the local community college or public school. If the classes are creative and touch on topics that older people are interested in, Builders will come and participate. Classes like these should have a non-churchy feel with no preaching, prayer, or pressure exerted. The object of the classes is to make a contact that can lead to further ministry in the future.[10]

Offer Counseling

Builders, of course, go through the same struggles as everyone else. They may suffer through boredom, depression, and anxiety. Older Builders have particular concerns that may not touch younger members of the population. As they make the transition into the last decades of life they often experience many losses: loss of a spouse, loss of income, loss of prestige, loss of driver's license, loss of home, and loss of health. To weather all of this loss, Builders would benefit from the counseling that churches can provide.

A major decision for an elderly Builder is when he or she should move to an apartment for senior citizens or even to a total care facility. Counseling can help the people involved make the decision and can help the elderly person adjust to his or her new home.

Be a Clearinghouse

Even if your church cannot provide many of the services mentioned here, consider becoming a clearinghouse where people can call to get information and referrals. Find out where people can turn when in need. Are there sources of home-delivered meals, low-cost transportation, and counseling? How do they locate elder-care facilities, medical help, and other services? Compile information on support groups for the elderly and for family members who are caregivers. Discover where people may turn for answers about daily medications, finances, and volunteer work. After you've compiled as much helpful information as possible, advertise your availability as a clearinghouse of information for people to call. You should consider printing a small handout for free distribution as a service to people in your community. For information on support groups near you, call the Self-Help Clearinghouse at (201) 625-7101.

Conclusion

Most people make commitments to Christ before they are adults. Believing in Christ with the faith of a little child becomes more difficult as one ages. A lifetime of ups and downs, broken relationships, and frustrated dreams makes it difficult for adults to freely consider the claims of Christ. Bob Saxe knows that churches can be effective in reaching Builders for Christ. As pastor to seniors at Bear Valley Baptist Church in Lakewood, Colorado, he has helped create a ministry that reaches out to unchurched Builders through various need-meeting ministries, such as transportation, help with filing income taxes, or completing forms for Medicare. In so doing, the people at Bear Valley have put feet on Christ's promise to help lift the burden when he said, "Come to Me, all who are weary and heavy-laden, and I will give you rest" (Matt. 11:28). They have discovered that Builders can and do make personal commitments to Christ as they experience the love of Christ demonstrated in practical, hands-on ways by Christians.

The Builder Generation

Aliases	Strivers Survivors Suppies (senior, urban professionals) Opals (older people with active lifestyles) Rappies (retired, affluent professionals) The War Babies (born 1940–1945) G.I. Generation Silent Generation Seniors
Formative Years	1920s, 1930s, and 1940s
Formative Experiences	World War I The Roaring Twenties The Great Depression Rural lifestyle The automobile Radio The New Deal Big bands Pearl Harbor and World War II Rationing The Korean War Family, school, and church
Characteristics	Hard workers Savers Frugal Patriotic Loyal Private Cautious Respectful Dependable Stable Intolerant

Religious Characteristics	Committed to church Support foreign missions Enjoy Bible study Loyal to denominations Minister out of duty Worship in reverence.
Builder Ministry	Provide group activities Sunday school Mission projects In-depth Bible study Focus on marriage and grandparenting Encourage contact with other generations Offer pastoral care Challenge them to pass on leadership
Common Areas of Concern	Financial concerns Affordable housing Personal safety Continued health Adequate transportation Preparation for death Spiritual needs Retirement options Substance abuse education Elder abuse education
Reaching Unchurched Builders	Set up hot lines Provide support groups Schedule traditional activities Help with social security and income taxes Sponsor trips Offer classes Offer counseling Train for grandparenting Be clearinghouse for Builder needs Offer respite care

Part 2

The Boomer Wave

4

Who Are the Boomers?

The early boom of babies following World War II was at first not surprising. A rise in the birth rate after the "boys came home" was expected. Within a few years, however, the staggering growth of 4 million babies a year alerted observers that something different was taking place. One thing was certain, the babies just kept coming and coming and coming. Between 1954 and 1964, more than 4 million births were recorded in the United States each year. Enough Boomer babies came to create a "pig-in-a-python" effect. As one can see the bulge of a pig moving through the digestive tract of a python, so the Boomer wave can be observed moving through society.

Advertisers were the first to catch on to the Boomer wave, which today represents one-third of the U.S. population. Marketers targeted Boomers' parents, who desired to give their children what they never had during the Great Depression. In 1958 alone, more than $100 million worth of Davy Crockett paraphernalia and $20 million worth of hula hoops were sold.

Boomers are the most educated generation in American history. They made heroes of John F. Kennedy and the Reverend Martin Luther King Jr. They rejoiced in the successes of NASA and the first men on the moon while struggling through the emotional ups-and-downs of Vietnam. They spawned and made a success of *American Bandstand* and the "Top Ten."

Of the three broad generations described in this book, the Boomers are the largest generation. They are the most studied, rebellious, independent, and affluent generation of the three. "Baby Boomer" technically refers to those people born between 1946 and 1964. In 1995 they are thirty-one to forty-nine years old and comprise approximately 76.5 million people, representing 30 percent of the United States population.

As with the other generations, Baby Boomers are not one homogeneous whole. They are a mosaic of subgroups as indicated by the numerous names given to this influential generation. Some of these names are Yuppies (young urban professionals), Dinks (double income, no kids), Thirtysomethings and Fortysomethings, Postwar Babies, and Postwar Generation. The name New-Collar workers is given to those in service-oriented jobs between the Yuppie and laboring ranks. Unnamed is a Boomer subpopulation of have-nots: unskilled workers, nonworking women with children, and heads of single-income households with incomes of less than $15,000 per year. Many of these have-nots are young couples whose combined incomes of $25,000 per year leave them struggling to pay the mortgage.

A descriptive name for this generation is Challengers.[1] The sheer number of Boomers has made them a challenge. In the 1950s the nation's school systems were forced to build thousands of new school buildings to house this new generational wave that was moving into kindergarten. Thousands of new teachers had to be trained to teach them. They challenged the tastes and styles of music as they embraced the Beatles and invented new dance styles.

In the 1960s when many of the Boomers were in their teens and twenties they challenged the morals, rules, and traditions of their parents, schools, and the government. With strong protests against the war in Vietnam and in favor of civil rights for African Americans, this decade became known as the turbulent sixties.

Today this largest generation in the history of the United States challenges our nation's economy to provide them with jobs and health care. And in the early 2000s they will challenge the ability of the social security system to provide the retirement income toward which they will have contributed for nearly fifty years.

The 76 million Boomers are at once a generation of wide diversity and uncanny similarities. Many of them came of age in a time when the United States moved from an industrial economy to one driven by the new information age. The rapid pace of change created a massive generation gap—unlike anything ever seen before—between them and their Builder parents. The formative decades for Boomers were the 1950s, 1960s, and 1970s.

The Boomer Generation can be divided into two primary groups: the Leading Edge—those born between 1946 and 1954—and the Trailing Edge[2]—those born between 1954 and 1964.

The Leading-Edge Boomers

There are roughly 34 million people who are Leading-Edge Boomers (LEBs). A vivid memory of many of these older Boomers is the gathering of 200,000 on the Washington Mall on August 28, 1963, when the Reverend Martin Luther King Jr. built an emotional plea for equality on the refrain "I have a dream." Leading-Edge Boomers were the leaders of change. These older Boomers cut their political teeth during a time of activism and optimism. Though still activists at heart, today they are concerned with saving for retirement, keeping and advancing in their jobs, paying off their mortgages, taking care of elderly parents, and putting kids through college.

Some Influential Leading-Edge Boomers

Connie Chung, 49
Bill Clinton, 49
Hillary Rodham Clinton, 48
Natalie Cole, 45
Andre Dawson, 41
Reggie Jackson, 49
Diane Keaton, 48
Robert Kennedy Jr., 41
Barbara Mandrell, 47
Dan Quayle, 48
Sylvester Stallone, 49
Clarence Thomas, 47
Donald Trump, 49
Denzel Washington, 41
Stevie Wonder, 45

Ages as of 1995

The Trailing-Edge Boomers

The second half of the Boomer Generation, born between 1955 and 1964, is called the Trailing Edge. There are about 42 million in this group. The Trailing-Edge Boomers (TREBs) were too young to be involved in the activism of the sixties. The two key events in their lives during the 1970s were the national energy crisis and the resignation of President Nixon following the Watergate scandal. Today they are concerned with getting established in a career, buying a house, and raising children. These younger Boomers have faced tougher competition for jobs because the older LEBs have often already filled the positions.

Several changes took place during 1954 and 1955 that

separate the LEBs and TREBs. For example, 1954 was the first year that a majority of American households had television. Older Boomers actually spent their first formative years with very little T.V. The polio vaccine was introduced in 1955, ending a disease that had terrified early Boomers. Polio had been eradicated by the time the later Boomers were in school, but they had other worries. As children they heard much about the dangers of environmental pollution.

Some Influential Trailing-Edge Boomers

Anita Baker, 37	Kenny G, 39
Charles Barkley, 32	Michael Jordan, 32
Bjorn Borg, 39	Bill Laimbeer, 38
LeVar Burton, 38	Spike Lee, 38
Dana Carvey, 40	John McEnroe, 36
Kevin Costner, 40	Akeem Olajuwon, 32
Tom Cruise, 33	Pam Shriver, 33
Dave Dravecky, 39	*Ages as of 1995*

Alice Kahn, writing in the *San Francisco Chronicle*, states that "the nightmare of disease that haunted the LEBs' childhood ended with a triumph from science and technology. The nightmare of the dying planet that the TREBs were raised with continues unabated."[3]

The early Boomers got the best education. They had more opportunities for good jobs than did younger Boomers because they entered the workforce at a time when the U.S. economy was expanding. Of course, they also faced the stress of the draft, the Vietnam War, and social unrest. In contrast, the younger Boomers faced deteriorating public education, cutbacks in college programs, and fewer job opportunities. Perhaps because opportunities have not been as plentiful for the TREBs as for the LEBs, TREBs seem to be more politically conservative. A study by the Times Mirror Center for the People and the Press reported in 1992 that age thirty-five "seemed to be the significant dividing point; below that age more people identify with the GOP while Democrats have an advantage among people thirty-five and over."[4]

Formative Experiences

The common self-awareness and sense of destiny among Boomers was created by the staggering impact of changes that took place during the 1950s, 1960s, and 1970s. Among the changes were several high impact events, which bonded Boomers into a generation set apart. These experiences stand in stark contrast to those that Builders experienced. Builders entered the world during a time of slow economic growth and its resulting depression. They faced wars and hardships that formed the work ethic and commitment characteristic of their generation.

Older Boomers, on the other hand, entered the world feasting on the victories and rising affluence following World War II. They moved through the first half of their lives literally on a forty-year binge fueled by industrial and consumer production.

The following helped to form the basic characteristics of the Boomer Generation.

Cold War

Cold War is a term coined to describe the hostility between the United States and the Soviet Union that endured from 1945 to 1989. It arose out of the failure of the two former allies to agree on the postwar restructuring of Europe and the Soviet Union's imposition of Communist governments on the nations of Eastern Europe. As children many Boomers lived in fear that the Communists would take over the world. The consequences of this were vague but terrible in their minds. Events such as the U-2 incident (1960), the Bay of Pigs invasion (1961), and the Cuban Missile Crisis (1962) reinforced these fears. Most of these events affected only the Leading-Edge Boomers and are just history to the TREBs. The Cold War ended with the fall of the Berlin Wall in 1989 and the collapse of the Soviet Union in 1991.

Television

In the 1950s there was a huge growth in the popularity of T.V. In 1950 there were 3.9 million households with T.V., growing to just over 30 million in 1955 and to 46 million in 1960. The growth in households with T.V. continued to escalate throughout the formative years of the Boomer wave. Its popularity and influence were evident when over 700 million people, the largest T.V. audience ever, watched the first men walk on the moon on July 20, 1969.

Programs like *Leave It to Beaver, Father Knows Best, Make Room for Daddy,* and *Ozzie and Harriet* were a few of the original shows that were popular during the early years of the Leading-Edge Boomers. Trailing-Edge Boomers growing up in the seventies watched programs that reflected the society of that era, such as *One Day at a Time.*

The growth of mass media, particularly television, has helped give the Boomers common interests and goals, even across economic lines. Dr. Ross Goldstein, a San Francisco psychologist and cofounder of Generation Insights, a consulting firm specializing in Boomer trends, says that similarities among Boomers are "partly because of the advent of television. It created a homogeneity in this generation that was unprecedented before."[5]

Economic Growth and Affluence

Builders grew up in difficult economic times. The Depression and World War II brought hard times that demanded sacrifice and a frugal lifestyle. In contrast, as Boomers grew up they seemed to float along easily as the U.S. economy boomed. At least one of the reasons for the baby boom was the plentiful jobs and growing wages that allowed families to have and support more babies.

Cheryl Russell reports on the economic growth of the early 1950s: "Median family income increased by more than $5000 during the 1950s and by more than $6000 in the 1960s, even after adjusting for inflation. In comparison, median family income did not increase at all during the 1970s, when the baby boom generation came of age."[6]

As Boomers began to get married and start families the old breadwinner husband and homemaker wife system began to break down. The increase in family income in the 1950s and 1960s was directly linked to that of the double-income family. It began to take two incomes to make ends meet. This move to a double-income family system forced a redefinition of marriage and family and stands as the most significant difference between the lifestyle of the Builders and that of the Boomers.

Education and Technological Growth

Following World War II educational opportunities expanded exactly at the time Boomers were born. The G.I. Bill opened education to thousands of returning soldiers from World War II, and education was heralded as the answer to society's ills. Boomers have known since they began reading *My Weekly Reader* that education was the pathway to success in life. Interestingly, it was at this time that education became what Professor Irving Kristol describes as the "adversary culture." As education began to stress issues of diversity and individual rights, it unwittingly became adversarial to the family, the church, and some feel, the nation as a whole. For example, the stress on individual rights now allows a child to sue his parents. This implies that the individual is more important than the family group.

Kristol notes, "It is hardly to be denied that the culture that educates us—the patterns of perception and thought our children absorb in their schools, at every level—is unfriendly (at the least) to the commercial civilization, the bourgeois civilization, within which most of us live and work."[7]

The growth of technology—particularly the transistor—transformed Boomer lifestyles. Nostalgic Boomers remember with fondness their first transistor radios, and Trailing-Edge Boomers remember the first video game—Pong—introduced in 1972 with sales of over 6,000 in its first year. The transistor literally changed our lifestyles, making possible everything from sophisticated kitchen appliances to automatic cameras, from digital watches to cars with transistorized ignitions.

The new technology produced new products that made life easier and more fun and improved products already available. More efficient automobiles and the construction of the nation's massive freeway system opened the way for the development of the suburbs. Automobile travel provided people a way to "see the USA in their Chevrolet," and the growth of airline travel literally brought the world closer to home.

Rock and Roll

Whereas Builders grew up on the sounds of swing and jazz music, Boomers cut their musical teeth on the new music style called rock and roll. No one, of course, popularized this new music form more than Elvis Presley. He rose to stardom singing a blend of blues and country western music. His sideburns, mannerisms, and attitude created what has become a cultural phenomenon. Songs like "Heartbreak Hotel," "Don't Be Cruel," "Love Me Tender," and "All Shook Up," along with concerts, television, and more than thirty movies, popularized a new style of music that continues to affect Boomer musical tastes. Other groups that Boomers remember include the Turtles, the Monkees, the Grateful Dead, and of course, the Beatles.

The climax of the rock generation's involvement with rock music came on August 15–17, 1969, when over 400,000 people gathered at a farm in Bethel, New York, for a concert showcasing the most famous performers of the times, including Jefferson Airplane, the Who, Jimi Hendrix, and Janis Joplin. The event combined a mixture of music, Vietnam War protest, and "good vibrations." Heavily covered by the media, it was depicted in the movie *Woodstock* in 1970 and became somewhat of a legend for many Boomers.

Civil Rights Movement

In 1955 Martin Luther King Jr., a Baptist minister, led a successful bus boycott to protest racial segregation in Montgomery, Alabama. Inspired by Mahatma Gandhi's philosophy of nonviolent civil disobedience, he founded the Southern Christian Leadership Conference in 1957 to combat segregation and racism.

Awakening the conscience of the United States, similar protests continued through the sixties. In 1957 the Civil Rights Commission was established to protect the African American right to vote. Later, the Civil Rights Act of 1964 prohibited discrimination in voting, education, hiring, and promotion of workers and guaranteed equal access to hotels, restaurants, theaters, and other public facilities.

The six-day Watts riot, August 11–16, 1965, was caused by long-term racial tensions and sparked by charges of police brutality. It resulted in thirty-four deaths and more than 1,000 injuries. Some 200 businesses were destroyed and property damage was estimated at $200 million. It alerted Boomers to the fact that legislative acts could not change the basic character of the nation. The protests, marches, and speeches stirred up the inward desire for justice in the minds of college-age Boomers and drew them into the national civil rights movement.

The New Frontier

During his presidential election campaign of 1960, John F. Kennedy called for a new frontier that would provide for federal aid for education, Medicare, equal opportunity in employment, and advances in space exploration. His call cast a dream of hope to a young generation that was tired of the Cold War and fear of Communism.

Having followed a president who was like a grandfather, JFK came roaring into the White House with a beautiful wife and preschool children! This "Camelot" presidency inspired widespread idealism and created an illusion that was never to be reality. The youthfulness of his family was a model for youthfulness in the sixties.

Kennedy's resounding statement, "Ask not what your country can do for you; ask what you can do for your country," became the trumpet charge for one of the most successful aspects of the new frontier policies—the Peace Corps. An overseas volunteer program still in existence today, the Peace Corps recruits volunteers who serve at the request of developing countries, usually for two years, in fields such as education, health care, and agriculture. Its goals are to help people and developing countries obtain basic necessities, promote world peace, and improve relations between the United States and the people of other countries.

Space Race

In 1958 the National Aeronautics and Space Administration (NASA) was founded to supervise U.S. space flights and activities beyond the earth's atmosphere. The agency focused on research and the building and testing of spacecraft. Its accomplishments include the launching of hundreds of satellites and space probes, and six successful moon landings.

As a part of JFK's new frontier, a mandate was given to place a man on the moon in the 1960s. NASA's crowning achievement occurred on July 20, 1969, when the Apollo 11 lunar module *Eagle* landed and Neil A. Armstrong first walked on the moon. The landing highlighted the hopes of Boomers, which were immortalized in Armstrong's words: "That's one small step for man, one giant leap for mankind." He later planted an American flag and left a plaque that read, "Here men from the planet Earth first set foot upon the moon July 1969 A.D. We came in peace for all mankind."

Assassinations

Actor Michael Douglas was in college in California. Kevin Kline was in high school in St. Louis. Jane Fonda was in Paris, filming a movie. Singers Peter, Paul, and Mary were en route to Dallas, to give a concert. All can recall precisely where they were and what they were doing on November 22, 1963, when they learned that President John F. Kennedy had been shot.

Oliver Stone's recent movie *JFK* sparked a new rise in assassination lore and a search for new clues to a possible conspiracy behind President Kennedy's death. Older members of the Boomer Generation seem particularly preoccupied with this assassination.

Actually three assassinations tarnished Boomer hopes and dreams: Kennedy in 1963, Martin Luther King Jr. in April 1968, and Robert Kennedy in June 1968. The impact of Kennedy's assassination on older Boomers was similar to that of Pearl Harbor on the Builder Generation. For African American Boomers, King's assassination also had long-lasting effects.

Vietnam War and Kent State

Boomers grew up in a time of social, racial, and artistic upheaval, and no experience characterized their turmoil more than the Vietnam War. It was the longest war that the United States has ever engaged in and the first in which we failed to achieve our goals.

Throughout the sixties popular demonstrations and political pressure to end the war mounted. Many Boomers in their twenties were strongly opposed to continued American involvement. "Tune in, turn on, and drop out" and "Hell, no, we won't go" were the battle cries. Following Richard Nixon's announcement on April 30, 1970, of the invasion of Cambodia and the need to draft 150,000 more soldiers for the Vietnam War, protesters staged antiwar rallies at Kent State University in Ohio. Governor James Rhodes ordered National Guardsmen to the university, where they used tear gas to disperse the crowd. When a shot was heard, the Guardsmen opened fire on the unarmed students, killing four and wounding nine. The incident incited massive protests across the country.

Energy Crisis

The Arab-controlled Organization of Petroleum Exporting Countries (OPEC) imposed restrictions on the United States and other industrialized countries in retaliation for their support of Israel during the Yom Kippur War in 1973. The embargo caused gas shortages leading to rationing, long gas lines, and higher prices for petroleum products. A national speed limit of 55 mph was imposed to help reduce gas consumption. It signaled to the Boomers that there were, in fact, limits to the planet's resources. People began to realize that resources could not go on being depleted without severe consequences.

Watergate and the Nixon Resignation

In May 1973 the Watergate scandal unfolded. On June 17, 1972, five men had been arrested for breaking into the Democratic National Headquarters at the Watergate apartment and office complex in Washington, D.C. The intruders had been hired by the Committee to Re-Elect the President. President Richard M. Nixon denied any involvement, but investigative reporting by Bob Woodward and Carl Bernstein of the *Washington Post* implicated him and led to the events culminating in his resignation. (They won the 1973 Pulitzer Prize for their stories and wrote the best-seller *All the President's Men,* which was made into a film.) On August 8, 1974, Nixon announced his resignation, becoming the first president to resign from office. Gerald Ford was sworn in as the new president the following day. He said, "Our long national nightmare is over," referring to the Watergate scandal. On September 8, 1974, President Ford pardoned Nixon for any crimes he may have committed in the Watergate affair. Many Boomers, because of policy decisions made concerning the Vietnam War, had begun to distrust American government. The Watergate scandal reinforced this lack of trust.

Characteristics

Like any large group of people, not all Boomers have the same beliefs or fit the same mold. Male and female, black and white, wealthy and poor, northern and southern Boomers may all have different views. The Leading-Edge Boomers tend to be the activists whose strongest formative memories focus on the assassinations of John Kennedy, Robert Kennedy, and Martin Luther King Jr.; the rise of the civil rights movement; and the Vietnam War. The Trailing-Edge Boomers were more strongly affected by the end of the war in Vietnam, Watergate, and the resignation of Richard M. Nixon. They cannot be rigidly grouped together. Yet, as advertisers have discovered, there are some basic, valid characteristics that the members of this generation share.

Educated

Boomers have attained the highest education levels of any generation. Nearly one quarter of them have earned a college degree, compared with only 9 percent of people over sixty-five.[8] Changes in teaching methods and insights into the needs of all people affected the education of Boomers during their formative years. These changes have led to increased tolerance in all areas of race, gender, age, and belief systems. Their higher level of education is a major reason why Boomers are so different from Builders. Cheryl Russell explains in *100 Predictions for the Baby Boom* that education determines "the way people live, how they vote, what they buy, and what they believe. American society has become more diverse and more accepting of diversity because more of its members are educated. This is why the Baby Boom forges new ways of life and why there cannot be—no matter how much some people may want it—a return to the simple traditions of the past."[9]

An example of this diversity is seen in Congress in the people who represent us. Those people used to be mostly white males over sixty. The impact of the Boomer Generation is that Congress now is comprised of people of diverse ages and races, both male and female.

"As Boomers move through middle age they will likely continue to be more socially liberal than their Builder parents but will grow more conservative on the issues of crime and safety."[10]

Media-Oriented

For better or worse, Boomers are the first generation to be raised on T.V. This nonstop influence united Boomers by a common "electronic" bond. Television shaped Boomers' values, turning them into a consumer market. Shows like *I Love Lucy, The Honeymooners, The Mickey Mouse Club,* and *American Bandstand* all provided common symbols, fads, and experiences unknown in times past. During the Boomers' formative years, money spent on T.V. advertising soared from $171 million in 1950 to more than $1.6 billion in

1960, increasing to $3.6 billion in 1970! By the time Leading-Edge Boomers reached eighteen, they had watched nearly 300,000 hours of commercials.

Radio also continued to have influence, primarily as a medium for music. Because radio programming is narrowly targeted to meet every musical taste, it still reaches Boomers today. They are not unlike other age groups who like radio because it holds their attention, moving quickly from one song to the next. It also costs less than other mediums and offers the freedom of listening while doing other things.[11]

Independent

Rapid changes during the information age taught Boomers that long-term relationships and commitment were going to be difficult to manage. Whereas their Builder parents may have grown up, gone to school, worked, and retired in the same town or geographical area, it has not been so for Boomers. Some Boomers stayed put during their childhood days, but they often went out of state for college or university. After graduating from college a Boomer often accepted a job in an entirely different geographic area. Once employed, many followed the legendary IBM (I've Been Moved) path to promotion. During the 1980s when Boomers were working their way up the ladders of success, 17.3 percent of the general population moved every year. Of the major age groups, those that moved the most were those twenty to twenty-nine and thirty to forty-four years old, or almost all Boomers. The average person moved once every three to five years during the 1970s and 1980s. Today, of course, there continues to be great mobility in our society, but it has slowed down since the seventies and eighties. IBM is now allowing its employees to remain in one location longer than was common in the fast-paced eighties.

For Boomers, mobility destroyed the normal networks of

relationships and commitments that are usually nurtured through many years of association. Many Boomers have not known the support of continuing relationships. They miss the commitments to church and work enjoyed by their parents. As they approach midlife they are feeling the need for friends and supportive networks. The years of having to uproot and separate from friends and personal commitments have taught them to hold long-term relationships and memberships at arm's length. For example, Boomers may join a health club a month at a time but rarely for a year or more. Similarly, some Boomers move from one church to another without concern.

Boomers are independent and tend to be less loyal than Builders to an employer or even to a church. Most vote for a person, not a party.

Forty years ago, people who were dissatisfied with their career choices simply accepted their lot in life. They stayed with ill-fitting jobs, earned their twenty-five-year pins or gold watch, and retired. Not so for Boomers. The idea of working twenty-five to thirty years for a gold watch is gone. As of 1992 about one in eight job changers abandoned his or her job voluntarily.[12] Most Boomers will experience three to six major career changes during their working years.

Cause-Oriented

The formative years of older Boomers were filled with causes. Whether it was fighting Communism or marching for civil rights, protesting against the war in Vietnam or volunteering for the Peace Corps, they pitched in and fought for what they believed in. Today Boomers are well represented in groups like MADD (Mothers Against Drunk Drivers), and they support such varied efforts as gay rights, pro-life, and preservation of the environment. Boomers still believe they must try to make the world better for everyone.

Fitness Conscious

As Boomers have moved toward middle age, many have tried to stay in good physical shape. They patronize health clubs and health food restaurants. Since the 1980s they have caused the sales of muscle-building machines like Nautilus to grow while taking up swimming, tennis, and even folk dancing in efforts to keep in shape.

There are far more recreational opportunities now than there were fifty years ago, and Boomers tend to enjoy participating in them. Hang gliding, indoor soccer, and sailboarding are just a few examples.

Rock Music Fans

Boomers still like music with a beat. The midlife resurgence of singers like Paul McCartney of the Beatles and Paul Simon and groups like the Moody Blues and the Beach Boys is directly related to the support of their aging Boomer fans.

As Boomers mature they are broadening their musical tastes, but they are not likely to give up the music they have enjoyed for a quarter of a century. One style of music that is attracting a larger Boomer audience is country music. Fifty percent of country music listeners are Boomers. Many Boomers also enjoy the same music as their Buster children. Boomers are least likely to listen to the two formats of big band/nostalgia and easy listening/beautiful music.[13]

Activists

An advertising brochure for the American Association of Boomers declares, "We are the generation that makes a difference." It begins with an open letter that reads in part, "When we were younger, we wanted to make a difference. Some of us worked within the system. Some of us fought against it. But we all wanted to make a difference. . . . We can make a difference." Boomers are activists. They still like to get involved, whether as part owners of the firms they work for or on the school board.

Quality Conscious

Boomers were given practically everything they wanted by parents who desired them to have what "we never had." Targeted by every major manufacturer and marketer for the past five decades, Boomers are used to quality products. The affluent fifties and sixties created a craving, even a feeling of entitlement, for nice things. It does not matter whether it is cars, baby strollers, or food; it has to be the best. Their children, the Baby Boomlet, have contributed to the growth of private schools in part because Boomer parents desire quality education for their children.

Question Authority

Due to the training they received from home, church, and the military, Builders rarely questioned any authority. Boomers, on the other hand, learned not to trust authority. The Vietnam War and Watergate scandal taught Boomers to distrust government, the military, and other forms of authority. In the sixties they used to say, "Don't trust anyone over thirty." Boomers are now over thirty, but they still find it hard to trust, being especially critical of politicians and people in authority.

Conclusion

Boomers have influenced our world since they first came on the scene. Think of the impact these Boomers have had: Bill Clinton, Reggie Jackson, Sylvester Stallone, and Christa MacAuliffe, to name a few. In the 1950s Boomers rode the waves of victory flowing from World War II and a growing economy. Then in the 1960s they enjoyed a "Camelot" dreamworld complete with hopes for world peace and brotherhood. By the 1970s they were retreating as the wall of Camelot came tumbling down into piles of disillusionment and cynicism. In the 1990s Boomers wonder what the future holds and how they will fare in the years to come when it looks as though there will be less money, more crime, more pollution, and children dependent on them longer than expected.

5

Boomer Believers

As we move toward the new millennium, the year 2000, we face a new era in human history. Unless Christ returns in the second half of the 1990s, the years following 2000 are not likely to be ones of peace, prosperity, and justice. But they will be ones of great opportunity for Christ's church.

The Lead Generation

Baby Boomers are members of what sociologists call the "lead generation." A lead generation tends to set the agenda for the entire nation. As the lead generation goes, so goes the nation—and the church. Local churches that are able to anticipate future directions and create solid strategies to deal with the Boomer wave will experience growth. Those that do not foresee and adapt to meet this challenge will find it increasingly difficult to minister effectively. The Boomer population in the United States alone is three times the population of Canada. Churches cannot afford to ignore them.

Writing in 1990 about the need for churches to understand and minister to Boomers, Dr. Elmer Towns reminds us that "the Boomer influence must be faced by the church. Within ten years they will take over the leadership of local churches and denominational headquarters." He continues, "When they take over the leadership of Christian organizations, they will functionally operate the church differently. To properly reach them, we must recognize the unique needs they bring to Christianity. Just as the church cannot reach the Chinese without understanding Chinese culture, values, and language, so the church must understand the Boomer in order to develop a cross-cultural strategy to reach and minister to the Baby Boomers in America."[1]

Some churches have found it difficult to attract and keep Boomers. Lyle Schaller was one of the first people to note the fact that churches were losing the Boomer Generation. In a 1985 article, "Whatever Happened to the Baby Boomers?" Schaller noted that "13 percent of the persons born in the 1955–64 era, the peak of the Baby Boom years, claim 'no church affiliation.' This contrasts to only 4 percent for those born in 1940 or earlier."[2]

A newer survey conducted between 1988 and 1992 by Dr. Wade Clark Roof presents a fresher perspective. Dr. Roof, the J. F. Rowny Professor of Religion and Society at the University of California in Santa Barbara, published his findings in *A Generation of Seekers* in 1993. Among other things, he discovered that of the 76 million Boomers about a third (25 million) never quit going to church. Of the two-thirds that did drop out of church, close to 40 percent have returned. Putting both of these groups together, there are roughly 45 million Boomers who are members of churches today. And of them about 58 percent, or 26 million, attend a church or synagogue on a regular basis. Not all, of course, attend Bible-believing churches. Dr. Roof divides these church attenders into two groups: "seekers" and "believers but not belongers."

He found that 28 percent of all Boomers are believers and 9 percent seekers who hop from faith to faith. Only 4 percent of Boomers say they are agnostics and 1 percent atheists.[3]

Boomers and Religion

The spiritual economy in the United States is changing just like its fiscal economy. As the 60s Generation matures, the Boomers' religious expression is more eclectic than ever. Throughout most of their lives many have simply ignored the church. While they may value it for its occasional social calls for justice, they have used the church primarily for hatching (baby dedications), matching (weddings), patching (counseling), and dispatching (funerals).

There are, however, some general religious perspectives around which churches can build ministries that will attract Boomers.

Commitment to Relationships

Boomers are sometimes characterized as uncommitted to church. Their interpersonal relationships tend to be weak, resulting in a high divorce rate and broken families. They resist joining organizations. These factors mean that Boomers relate to the church differently than their parents did. The Me Generation wants a personal relationship with God, not a set of rules. Corporately they want relationships with each other that are based on open and honest understanding of how people think and feel.

In practice the Builder Generation's commitment to Christ was expressed through involvement with the institutional church. They gave their time, energy, and money to church. A common statement heard from Builders is, "Whenever the doors of the church were open, we were there." In contrast, Boomers see their commitment to Christ as a personal thing, not measured by church attendance. A Builder husband might ask his wife, "Do you think we should go to church tonight?" His wife would reply, "Yes, the church needs our support, and we need to set a good example for the children." If a Boomer husband asked his wife the same question, his wife might answer, "No, I think it best that we stay home this evening. We haven't had much time together as a family, and I think it is important that we spend some time with the children." Both couples may be equally committed to Christ, but Builders tend to interpret commitment to Christ as equal to church attendance. Many Boomers believe that their church attendance does not reflect the degree of their commitment to Christ.

Church Membership

The independence of Boomers is evident in the way they change their religious affiliation. While Builders tend to remain committed to the denomination of their youth, many Boomers have changed religious affiliation at least once. According to a poll conducted by the Princeton Religion Research Center, "Nearly 25 percent of U.S. adults have changed their religious affiliation at least once, with conversion to Protestantism being nine times more common than conversions to Catholicism." Reportedly, 19 percent left Baptist churches, 11 percent left Methodist churches, and 6 percent left Presbyterian churches.[4] Many researchers have noted that most of those who change appear to be Boomers. Since Boomers often move easily from one denomination to another, people are seeing less value in denominational names than they did before. Many churches decide not to use their denominational name in signs and public advertising.

One of the reasons Boomers often do not follow in their parents' footsteps in choosing a church is because they are more mobile, moving on the average of once every three to five years with only about a fifty-fifty chance of attending a church of the same denomination they left. Boomers are attracted to churches that have celebrative and participative worship services with contemporary music. The church has become for them a way station or stopover on their spiritual pilgrimage.

People Not Programs

A general misconception surrounding Boomers is that they will not contribute money to a church. On the contrary, Boomers are not as egocentric as one might assume. Like all generations, as Boomers have aged, they have substantially increased their giving to charitable organizations, and now they are entering their peak earning years. Many are also inheriting money from Builder parents.

Perhaps because they are better educated, Boomers are sophisticated in handling money and tend to think carefully before investing it. Since they are concerned for causes and are highly relational, they want to give money to organizations that prove they are actually doing something of great value for people. They look for a return on their investment, and they want to see the results of their investment firsthand.

In the church this is seen in the desire of Boomers to support projects and people who are close to home, since it's easier to see results in local ministries.

Living Their Faith

Boomers appreciate those who honestly live their faith as opposed to just wearing it on Sundays. They tend to be down-to-earth and think nothing of calling their pastor by his first name or wearing jeans and tennis shoes to church.

Boomers favor activism. They want to get involved and are usually open to ministry in the local church. They view themselves as problem solvers, but they will not minister purely out of a sense of duty or responsibility. They are just too busy for that. Ministry must fit their interests, needs, and sense of fulfillment. "Boomers are looking for action," writes Dr. Roof. "They are also looking for an identity, and churches with clear-cut beliefs and boundaries are best able to supply that."[5] They want vitality and movement in the institutions they participate in, especially the church. Large churches that have a lot going on often meet these needs because the participants sense that ministry is happening.

Experimenting

Much of the Leading-Edge Boomers' time in the sixties was spent experimenting—with drugs, causes, communes, and music. Many have also experimented with religion, trying out Eastern religions, EST, self-help philosophies, and New Age cults. Those who are Christians bring their desire to experiment to the worship service. They have enjoyed singing and clapping to praise songs and bringing drama and dance into the service. Hugs and "high five" affirmations are often enjoyed by this generation.

Tolerant of Differences

During the first fifty years of the twentieth century, people tended to see everything as either black or white, true or false, pure or impure. There was no in-between. In the latter half of this century, Boomers in general tend to see things in shades of gray rather than in black and white. They seem to have a greater tolerance for different viewpoints, lifestyles, and ideals. In the *Christian Education Journal* pastor Leith Anderson writes, "Especially frustrating to many senior pastors is the Baby Boomer's high tolerance of contradictions." Later he expands on this theme, noting, "It can be a frustrating phenomenon for a pastor to minister to parishioners who affirm the authority of the Bible and are active members of conservative churches, but who hold liberal views on cohabitation, divorce and remarriage, materialism, drugs, and alcohol. Even if the Boomer does not personally live with seeming contradiction he or she may be much more tolerant than his or her parents toward the differing views of others."[6]

Ministering to Boomer Believers

"Traditional Christian denominations will have their chance for growth and resurgence during the new decade," writes James Scudder of the Gannett News Service. "But only if they become less stodgy and bend to meet the real personal needs of people who come to them."[7]

Church attendance among Boomers, particularly older ones, is on the rise. At 42 percent of those born between 1946 and 1958, the rate is close to the percentage of their counterparts during the Depression era.[8] Middle-aged Boomers seem to be returning to many of our country's traditional values. Many LEBs are making their way back to churches. This will probably also be true of TREBs as they enter middle age.[9]

Although many Boomers are looking for spiritual renewal in their lives, they are not always returning to the denominations they attended as children. A study reported in *Progressions,* a Lilly Endowment Occasional Report, summarizes what is happening among returning Boomers.

> In general, the Boomers are seen as "consumers" looking to get something specific from a church, should they choose to join one. They are fussier (or more discriminating) than were their parents and will shop around to find the preacher, the spiritual atmosphere or the church school believed to fulfill their needs. They are—by general agreement of those who study them—not only picky, but highly pragmatic. Those who go back to church look

> for two things in particular: religious education for their children and some kind of religious experience that helps them make sense of their own lives.[10]

The following are some specific ways a church can attract and keep the Boomer Generation.

Highlight Purpose and Vision

Boomers often find churches dull and lacking excitement. They are attracted to a church that has a clearly stated purpose supported by specific plans. Remember, Boomers belong to a generation that fights for causes. They have led antiwar, human rights, and world hunger efforts. They need to know that a church has a vision of what God wants it to be and do.

John F. Kennedy left a legacy of activism to Boomers that caused them to focus on changing their world. As they've matured, they've turned their activist interest toward local issues. Churches that can cast a vision of ministry in areas close to home will be able to capture the interest and commitment of the Boomer.

Plan Celebrative Worship Services

Churches that perpetuate a traditional model of worship may find it difficult to keep Boomers. Those who leave traditional churches are often attracted to churches that have celebrative and participative worship services with contemporary music. Many Boomers find celebrative services meaningful because they are involved in the worship experience.

Celebrative services usually emphasize great themes of the faith, praise and worship, and congregational participation. They are fast paced, well planned, and rehearsed. Small bands often provide the accompaniment for the praise songs.

The traditional sermon format may not reach Boomers who have become used to the short, entertaining bursts of information provided by television. Consider the following:

- Stress practical application, not just content, in preaching and Bible teaching.
- Make sermons no longer than thirty minutes.
- Use a variety of teaching methods. Experiment with drama productions and video to illustrate the truths of Scripture.

Stress Quality

Boomers have higher expectations than their Builder parents of quality in programming, facilities, child care, and music in their churches. Lyle Schaller observes, "A new generation of people have come on the scene who expect attractive nurseries, air-conditioning, excellent acoustics, convenient off-street parking, carpeted rooms, comfortable chairs, attractive rest rooms, and many other amenities of life that were considered luxuries in the earlier years of the 20th century."[11]

Boomers understand that a church is not a business, but they want it to be businesslike in terms of quality and efficiency. They expect good business practices in the handling of finances and long range planning and understand how computers, fax machines, and cellular phones can aid a church's ministry.

Streamline Structure

The typical week for an average Boomer has very little uncommitted time. Sixty percent of middle-aged Boomers are parents, and two-thirds of Boomer wives work outside the home, compared to about half in the rest of the population. Boomer children are involved in after-school sports and activities. Work that was often done during the day twenty years ago—for example, grocery shopping and housecleaning—now must be done on the "second shift" after working partners come home. Two-income parents scramble to catch up with chores at night and on weekends. Though they may want to be involved in the church, they do not have large blocks of time that they can commit.

Streamline your church structure, eliminating useless positions, committees, and boards. Evaluate programs and use only those proven to be successful. Cluster several events together so people can have fewer nights out. For training, use weekend retreats and short seminars that do not require long-term attendance. Schedules should be made with commuters, working women, and dual-earner households in mind.

Recruit people based on their gifts rather than your church's need and recruit for shorter periods of commitment. Boomers have found that it works well to delegate decisions to small groups of concerned people who have the authority and responsibility to act. Boomers are more apt to be involved in programs if they have participated in the decision making.

Multiple Options

It was a 31-Flavors-Baskin-Robbins world that Boomers grew up in, and they continue to enjoy nearly unlimited choice in everything from food to entertainment. Shopping centers with hundreds of stores under one roof and acres of parking are now the norm. Superstores offering clothing, groceries, and hardware are becoming popular. Restaurants with a variety of cuisines line every city's main streets. And entertainment is cheap and varied through videos and cable T.V.

It's not surprising, then, that Boomers are attracted to churches that offer a variety of programs, ministries, and services. They expect ministries geared to various age groups, small group Bible studies, and preschools.

Smaller churches can attract Boomers by concentrating on the ministries and programs they do best, making sure they are high quality. They should establish one or two specialized ministries and then add new ministries on a gradual basis only when they can be done in a quality manner.

Use Small Groups

Place a healthy emphasis on relationships through the development of small group ministries. Boomers tend to like small groups because of their interest in the personal application of teaching and in relationships. This could mean that Boomers would choose to do Bible study in groups that do not meet on Sunday morning and are not content-oriented, as traditional adult Sunday school classes are. Groups that discuss issues, minister to personal needs, and offer close relationships often appeal to Boomers.

Restructure Existing Services

Some services in traditional churches could be restructured so that they would be more attractive to Boomers. For example, churches have traditionally held two worship services on Sunday, one in the morning and one in the evening. The morning service uses the varsity team. The congregation will hear the best musicians, the best sermons, and the best drama. The second string is brought in for Sunday evening. For this service, the pastor's sermon is not as well prepared, and the musicians are often people who need a little more practice before playing in the morning service. The entire evening service seems to drop down a notch or two in terms of quality.

Boomers, who are time and quality conscious, may not support such a service. Some churches have restructured the evening service by building in time for families, sponsoring a Bible institute in the same time slot, organizing small groups to meet in homes, and even moving adult education to Sunday evenings. In the last few years, some have started experimenting with worship services on Friday and Saturday evenings with good success.

Communicate Visually

Boomers are a visual generation. Raised on T.V., Boomers like to see as well as hear the message of the gospel. A trend that began to develop in the late sixties and has blossomed over the years is the projection of worship songs on a screen. When people look up at a screen, they raise their heads and sing out louder. A natural extension of the projection of songs in a worship service is the use of video. It is a rare church that does not have video equipment for use in the children's or youth department. Adult small groups often use Christian videos for teaching or Bible study. Coming, but not in large use yet, is video in the main worship services of the church. Some pioneering churches have started using video as a means of giving announcements during worship services and as a creative way to illustrate the pastor's message.

Related to all this is the use of small dramas during worship. These short (about five-minute) dramas draw people into the theme of the worship service in very powerful and personal ways. They fit the Boomer Generation well since they offer a visual experience of the message.

Expand the Roles of Women

Women are greatly influencing our society. Today, more than 1.3 million women age thirty-seven or younger hold managerial or administrative positions in business. The number of companies in the United States owned or controlled by women has grown to the point where they now employ more people than do all the Fortune 500 companies. The actual number of female-owned businesses grew 20 percent in 1992 to more than 6.5 million.[12]

Churches are wise not to waste this valuable resource. Take seriously the gifts, talents, calling, and proven ability of women. Create new ministries that will challenge and use the gifts of your women members. Schedule church services and meetings to fit working women's time constraints. Develop courses and seminars that will speak to the needs of women. Show your women members that you take them seriously by hiring a director of women's ministry.

Focus on Local Ministries

LEBs spent a great deal of their lives trying to change society. They focused on the big issues of life such as civil rights and world peace. Looking back they question whether much was accomplished, and in frustration, many prefer to focus their ministry efforts in local arenas, where they feel they have more control and can see the results of their work.

Churches can take advantage of this by developing and emphasizing ministries that are "over here" rather than "over there." Churches can focus on the needs in their immediate neighborhoods and the concerns important to their community and then organize efforts to meet some of these concerns.

Offer Short-Term Missions Involvement

Boomers, of course, can also develop interest in overseas missions, especially if they become personally involved.

James F. Engel, writing in *Christianity Today,* declares, "If international vision is to be expanded, direct exposure and involvement overseas is an absolute necessity; short-term service is the key to the problem." He goes on to say, "Our data from the Wheaton Graduate School study clearly demonstrate that those who have been involved overseas, even for a brief visit, have significantly greater awareness of the commitment to world evangelization."[13] Boomers may not give a lifetime to missions, but they may be willing to serve for a short time. Parachurch ministries have found that Boomers were willing to serve upon graduation from college for two to ten years, after which they have gone into other careers.

Conclusion

Churches that minister effectively to Boomers take seriously Boomer values, needs, and concerns. For example, since Boomers are experience-oriented, churches will take pains to provide ways for Boomers to experience Christianity. Since Boomers are future-oriented, churches must focus on tomorrow more than yesterday. Since Boomers are growth-oriented, a church must look beyond current membership to those who do not yet believe. Since Boomers are people-oriented, churches must be less concerned with programs and facilities and more concerned with the needs of people. And since Boomers are action-oriented, churches must do rather than just discuss.

In *Baby Boom Believers*, author Mike Bellah warns us that "the baby boom is simply too big and too influential to be ignored. Industries have been made or broken by the baby boom. Businesses have learned the hard way that you neglect the baby boom at your own peril."[14] Churches that want to grow must not ignore the Boomer Generation but adjust their ministries to attract and keep them.

6

Reaching the Boomer Generation

A Texas-based group—the American Association of Boomers (AAB)—was organized in June 1989 to channel the clout of 76 million Boomers. Modeled after the American Association for Retired Persons (AARP), AAB's goal is to advance the social, professional, and economic status of Boomers. They expect to have more than 1 million members by 1995.[1]

Several newsletters have been launched in an attempt to harness the tremendous power of Boomers. *Boomerang* was started by editor Jo-Ann Fitzgerald Conroy to provide information of interest to this generation and a forum for discussing issues such as the environment, economy, family, job changes, and the stress of dual-income marriages.

The American Association of Boomers also publishes a newsletter, *My Generation*, which covers political, financial, and social issues such as health care. A sample of articles includes titles such as "The AARP Is Picking Our Pockets" and "Boomers in the Electronic Age—Tapping Our Electronic Power."

Boomers are beginning to wield a huge amount of political clout. In past years, when Boomers were preoccupied with their professions and personal lives, Builders had a disproportionate influence in local elections. Boomers have been cynical about politics, and this too has kept them from voting. In 1989, however, Boomer voters began to control the outcomes of many local elections across the United States. Writing about Boomer influence on the Seattle city elections in 1989, Walter Hatch notes that "younger voters torpedoed all of those candidates. . . . This may be the first time that younger voters have controlled the outcome of a local election."[2]

Today more than half of all households are headed by a person born between 1946 and 1964. They will have $18 billion in discretionary income during the 1990s. "Politicians and marketing experts," writes Charles Colson, "are busily identifying the yuppies—where they live, what they eat, what kind of ads they respond to. But who in the church is doing this? All too often we tend to think in sermon-to-sermon strategy, rather than to look long-range at the ways we will reach those who need to hear the Good News."[3]

As Boomers are entering midlife they are becoming more open to spiritual things. Sadly their spiritual needs are often being met by the New Age movement rather than by the Christian church. There are indications that unchurched Baby Boomers are open to the gospel. How can we effectively reach them in the coming years?

Growing Spiritual Openness

Sociologist Charles Schewe of the University of Massachusetts states, "I don't expect yuppies to live forever as yuppies. As they age, have families and take on new responsibilities there will be a new lifestyle, a new look and a new value system for them."[4]

"Until now," writes Richard Eisenberg, "the major objectives of this generation have been short term: Find a job. Hook up with a mate. Start a family. Buy a house. Get a VCR. By age forty, many baby Boomers may well have reached most of these goals. But between forty and fifty, for what's likely to be the first time, you must take a truly long view."

The oldest Boomers will turn fifty in 1996, a strange thought for a generation that once declared they would not trust anyone over thirty. This is forcing them to come face-to-face with the second half-century of their lives. Menopause looms in the immediate future for many Boomer women. Wrinkles, balding, and heartburn cannot be far away. The new three Rs for Boomers are Reeboks, Rogaine, and Retin-A. Their new battle cry may be "Gray is good."

A survey of 1,600 Boomers concerning their church attendance found that about 33 percent can be labeled loyalists, never having left organized religion. Twenty-five percent can be labeled returnees, those who have come back to church. But the largest group, 42 percent, left church and have still not returned, although they have spiritual leanings. Further, Boomers can be divided into "mystics" and "theists." The mystics see God within themselves and are attracted by New Age teachings. The theists see an eternal source of spiritual authority, though not necessarily the God of the Bible.[5] Leading-Edge Boomers, who grew up in the counterculture of the 1960s, tend to be the ones who believe all religions are equally good. It is the Trailing-Edge Boomers—who actually attend church less—that are the more religious in the traditional sense.[6] Here are some indications that Boomers are slowing down for God.

Traditional Values

A national telephone survey of 1,000 Boomers by the American Council of Life Insurance found that young Americans want stronger family and religious ties. They desire a greater respect for authority and stricter moral values. Concerns about morals and religious training for their children appear to be major reasons for older Boomers to return to church. These concerns are not the only reasons, however. Many Boomers are asking very deep questions about their lives. For nearly three decades Boomers did not take seriously the institution of marriage. It was free love in the sixties, finding oneself in the seventies, and searching for success in the eighties. It appears that now many Boomers are headed back to the traditional home. "The 1990s is going to be the decade of the couple. We'll see that relationships can't be taken for granted anymore," says Dr. Samuel Pauker, one of more than fifty experts surveyed by *Bride's* magazine.[7]

The nineties will be a more grown-up era for Boomers. The reason? They are moving into middle age. The values they had in the sixties no longer satisfy as they have matured. Ann Clurman, vice president of Grey Advertising, expands on the Boomer search for values. "There is a free-floating sense of searching for a value system. All the instincts of the baby Boomers are saying, 'Slow down. Figure out what's important.' But they haven't arrived at what that is."[8]

Loss of a Fantasy

Since 1983 when the term "yuppie" first appeared in print, more than 22,000 articles have been written on the subject. In reality very few Boomers fit the profile of a Yuppie. Only about 5 percent of the Boomer population made the grade of age (young), income (high), geography (urban), attitude (selfish), and affections (BMWs).

But, of course, almost all had the fantasy—built on the concept of generational entitlement rooted in the prosperity of the fifties and sixties. The idea of having it all appealed to almost the entire generation. In a sense, yuppiedom was the natural outgrowth of the hedonism of the 1960s and the obsessive meism of the 1970s. Its materialism filled a void left by the neglect of God and traditional values.

By 1986 some declared that the Yuppie was dead. The death was brought about by family, finances, and fatigue. The wanton consumption—the getting-and-spending—frenzy of the early 1980s came to a halt with the arrival of the recession. Gone for most are the Mercedes and his-and-her Rolexes. With corporate cutbacks businesses have said good-bye to middle managers, and many Boomers face cutbacks in their materialistic lifestyles. The lavish upscalers of the eighties are now the frugal downscalers of the nineties. BMWs are traded for Fords (well, at least Hondas), and credit cards are cut up. The instincts of the Boomer today say, Slow down and find out what's important.

Slower Lifestyle

Commuter marriages and job transfers causing uprooting of families are by-products of a high-pressure, success-oriented lifestyle. This was exciting when Boomers were younger but has taken its toll on couples who have not had the time and energy to cement their marriages and families together. Deep down Boomers are hurting. Wade Clark Roof says, "We are all leading lives of quiet desperation. There is definitely a reclaiming of spirituality among many Boomers involved in what is at least in part a midlife quest for meaning."[9]

An article in *USA Today* titled "Baby Boomers Hit Brakes after Life in the Fast Lane" details how the changing marriage and growing family are slowing down Baby Boomers to a more serious pace of life. Those Boomers who can afford it and are willing to take the career risk are moving to communities with less stress, crime, smog, and people. Interestingly enough, they want a nice quiet place to raise their kids. At the same time they are beginning to think seriously about the spiritual life of their families.

Dr. Melvyn Kinder suggests in his book *Going Nowhere Fast* that Boomers want to get off seven different treadmills:

- The Ambition Treadmill
- The Money Treadmill
- The Personal-Appearance Treadmill
- The Sexual-Performance Treadmill
- The Waiting-for-Love Treadmill
- The Marriage/Divorce Treadmill
- The Raising-Perfect-Children Treadmill

Job Competition and Finances

July 20, 1988, was a significant date to demographers. On that date, the group of those aged thirty-five to fifty-nine equaled and began to exceed the size of the eighteen to thirty-four-year-old group. As Boomers move through middle age, this older portion of the population will become its fastest growing segment. Right now the number of young workers is declining and the number of prime-age employees is exploding. In effect, "everyone who will be working in the year 2000 has already been born, and two-thirds of them are at work today."[10]

As businesses downsize, old jobs are eliminated as new jobs open up, often forcing middle-aged Boomers back into the job market. Younger Boomers are advancing up the promotion ladder, and since older workers expect more in terms of benefits and compensation, employers are often willing to replace them with younger and less costly workers, even Baby Busters just entering the job market.

Burdened with mortgages and family costs, prime-aged Boomers face stresses they never encountered before. The American Dream traditionally included finding a good job, purchasing a home, and raising a happy family. Sometimes included in the dream were Mom at home full-time, a large yard with a dog, and piano lessons and good schools for the kids. During most of the history of the United States, an unwritten rule of the American Dream was that the standard of living of each succeeding generation would surpass that of its parents. For most Baby Boomers this may not be possible, due to the changing nature of our economy. A recent television ad for an investment firm shows a young couple asking why they can't buy a home and go on vacations the way their parents did. "The baby boom's greatest asset, its size, has become its greatest liability. Its size has caused it to face the real possibility of becoming the first generation in American history that may not expect to equal the living standards of its parents."[11] *Money* magazine reports a study by Lawrence Eisenstein, a New Jersey psychiatrist, who asked 1,300 middle-aged people to name their greatest concern. Seventy percent replied "having enough money to cover expenses." Common fears were having to support aging parents, getting divorced or outliving their spouses, supporting stepchildren, and paying for children's college education. Many Boomers bought homes during inflationary times and, in fact, "have merely been treading water," writes Frank Levy of the University of Maryland.

A high-spending group, Boomers are just beginning to think about retirement. With little trust in social security, many are beginning to worry about having enough for a comfortable retirement. Most analysts project that the social security program is sound until around 2030, but after that no one is quite sure what will happen. Boomers wonder if it will be sound that long.

Boomers are not saving the way their parents did. The average personal savings of a Baby Boomer is $1,200. A survey by TIAA-CREF in 1993 reported that "54 percent of Baby Boomers aged 25 to 44 . . . said they didn't feel financially prepared for retirement. It also reported that Baby Boomers now set aside an average of only a third of the amount they'll need to maintain their preretirement standard of living."[12]

Reevaluating Goals

The zest for corporate battle that was exhilarating to the thirty-year-old manager often seems empty and futile to the forty-five-year-old executive. Over 60 percent of career people are "working wounded." The Vietnam War forced many young men to move into careers with only the thought of not being drafted. Women wonder if working outside the home is worth the personal sacrifices they've had to make. As a result, many Boomers are heading back to school and starting second careers, all the while reevaluating their work, family, and personal development. Midlife Boomers often realize that jobs have taken them far away from old friends and family members. Thus, they are redefining *family.* Family to many Boomers is any group of people whose members love and care for each other.

As Boomers move into middle age, they are realizing that the materialistic "me" approach is not satisfying. They are beginning to work together. Their top concerns for the nineties are ethics, environmentalism, and meaningful experiences, all of which can best be accomplished together. Out with the "me" generation; in with the "we" generation is the new view. Now there is discussion of the value of self-fulfillment versus responsibility, individual ambition versus the needs of others, living together versus marriage, and liberal social values versus conservative social values.

Maturity

Boomers are growing up. A reflection of the Boomer maturation is evident in the new music being sung by rock stars who grew up with the Boomers, like Bruce Springsteen, James Taylor, and Eric Clapton. These headliners are still doing tours, but today Springsteen, 42, sings about fatherhood, Taylor, 44, about the devastated environment, and Clapton, 47, about the death of his son.

Marketers are beginning to target an aging Boomer Generation with new products designed specifically for them. Maybelline, for example, is in hot pursuit of aging Boomers. With an $8 million advertising budget in 1993, Maybelline launched a new line of makeup for women aged thirty-five and older. Using "age-appropriate" models, they sell their new age-denying makeup, called Maybelline Revitalizing.

Reaching Unchurched Boomers

As Boomers have moved through the normal stages of life they have come to realize that there is no salvation in secular society. Now as many of them enter midlife, part of their midlife crisis is an intensifying search for meaning.

Faith is coming to bear on the lives of Boomers, but they still shy away from organized religion. At the heart of their search for faith, notes sociologist Wade Clark Roof, is a deep yearning for "meaning and belonging. There is a kind of spiritual renewal occurring among members of this generation," writes Roof, "but it does not necessarily mean a return to organized religion."[13]

A generation ago religion was considered to be a very private matter. Today many choose lifestyles closely aligned with religious beliefs. Jimmy Carter, Jesse Jackson, Charles Colson, and Ronald Reagan serve as models for many. Churches can effectively reach Boomers as they strategically target their outreach ministries to meet Boomer needs and interests.

Emphasize Family

As Boomers have aged, they have become more intensely involved with their children. Since 1992 several new magazines have been launched that highlight growing family needs and interests. Jann S. Wenner, who founded *Rolling Stone* over a quarter century ago and became a leading voice of the Boomer Generation, plans to publish a new magazine for his peers. Titled *Family Life,* it will be aimed at parents in their thirties and forties with children under twelve years old. Original circulation is expected to be about 300,000.

Wenner was not the first to recognize the new Boomer interest in families or to start a magazine aimed at them. Almost four years ago, Jake Winebaum started *Family Fun* magazine. Hearst Magazines is producing *Family Adventures,* a travel publication that targets parents and their children five to fifteen years old. Recognizing that there are about 38 million adults with children in this age group, they are betting that Boomers are now ripe for this type of magazine.

These magazines deal with topics that are now of interest to Boomers, but they can't meet the deep needs of Boomers. In fact, no other institution has the resources to offer Boomer families that churches do. Marriage and family ministries have long been the foundational ministries for many churches. Churches have the knowledge and resources to lead searching Boomers into lifelong commitments, healthy child rearing, and strong family units. But churches must take their knowledge into the marketplace by offering seminars and workshops on parenting in the community. Unchurched Boomers are not likely to walk into a Sunday school class on parenting.

Develop Bridge Ministries

There is a need for "bridge ministries" to help unchurched Boomers move into a church. Bridge ministries focus on building relationships with unchurched people in the community to help these people ease into the church. Some areas to target:

- Consider offering career guidance. Many Boomers are changing careers and may need help identifying their abilities, their goals, and their passions. Offer courses in career planning to help Boomers retool for the future.
- Start small groups for stepparents. A high divorce rate and an equally high remarriage rate have led to a dramatic increase in the number of stepfamilies in our communities. The Stepfamily Association of America estimates that 1,300 new stepfamilies are being formed every day in the United States. There are some 35 million stepparents. A study of remarried couple households published by Johns Hopkins University reported that 10 percent of all children under eighteen years old are living in a stepfamily.
- Why not try a divorce recovery workshop or an out-of-work support group or a parents-of-AIDS-victims support group? A preschool and an elementary school; a singles ministry; support groups for those combating drug addiction, alcoholism, or homosexuality; marital counseling and marriage enrichment seminars are

other types of ministries that could serve as bridges to the unchurched Boomer.

Develop a Seeker Service

A large number of churches have found that the addition of a second worship service targeted directly to Boomers is a successful way to reach them with the gospel. A seeker service should

- Use contemporary music.
- Stress praise/worship.
- Allow participation, such as clapping.
- Use audio/visual media.
- Use Scripture from a modern translation.
- Print first-class bulletins.
- Encourage conversation before and after the service.
- Limit preaching to twenty to thirty minutes.
- Stress practical living.
- Provide alternate ways to acknowledge acceptance of Christ, such as with decision cards. (Do not ask Boomers to come forward during the service.)

It's important to make guests feel welcome. Enter the door of a Wal-Mart store, and you will be greeted by a friendly person who offers you a shopping cart. Wal-Mart understands the need to greet guests graciously, and their success has prompted competitors such as Target and K-Mart to follow suit.

To welcome Boomer guests

- Give them the best parking.
- Give them the best seats.
- Hold worship services at convenient times.
- Provide a visitors center.

- Use trained greeters.
- Offer a welcome packet of valuable information.
- Make good use of directional signs.
- Provide a fellowship time after worship that makes guests feel welcome.
- Welcome them from the pulpit but do not have them stand and speak.

Stress Lifestyle Evangelism

Train members to develop friendships with the unchurched and give them time to do it by limiting the number of church activities. Organize nonthreatening events such as parties and concerts to which the unchurched can be invited. Valentine banquets, harvest dinners, and Sunday school picnics can all be planned to help make the unchurched feel comfortable.

Members should invite friends to worship services. Lyle Schaller describes congregations that effectively invite Boomers to church:

> The congregations in which members invite others to come to church with them usually display these characteristics: a) members are enthusiastic about their faith, b) members are enthusiastic about their congregation, c) members are enthusiastic about the current pastor, d) the congregation, as a whole, conveys the expectation that members will invite others, e) most members actively and enthusiastically greet and welcome visitors, f) the worship experience is planned with the assumption that first-time visitors will be present.[14]

Build on the desire for relationships by developing small groups. Use a combination of Bible studies, fellowship groups, social groups, task groups, accountability groups, and support groups. Don't forget the draw of sports for both men and women. Boomer women enjoy fitness, and many of them will be attracted to co-ed volleyball teams, aerobics classes, and jogging groups. Reliance on one type of group, such as Bible studies, will usually not work. Give Boomers multiple choices.

Provide Quality Child Care

Boomers expect a church nursery to be comparable to their baby's room at home. They want a church nursery to provide the same quality care they would find at the best weekday care centers. Churches hoping to reach Boomers should improve church nurseries with good lighting, new carpeting, clean toys, and bright colors. Nurseries should be accessible and well staffed, with well thought-out policies.

Have a well-structured program for elementary-aged children, using up-to-date materials and methods. Replace closed Sunday school rooms with learning centers.

Offer Opportunities for Service

"We are the generation that makes a difference" declares the headline on a brochure from the American Association of Boomers. Inside it begins, "When we were younger, we wanted to make a difference." Boomers have long had a desire to serve others. Think of ways you might be able to involve unchurched Boomers in your church ministries. Of course, there are places of service that are inappropriate for an unchurched person to serve, such as a Sunday school teacher or board member, but there may be places where they can serve and build a relationship with your church, which could lead to their hearing and receiving the gospel. Be sure to

- Recruit through personal contact.
- Ask for short commitments.
- Emphasize team ministry and play down superstar ministry.
- Provide training.

Get Involved in Your Community

Many, if not most, of today's churches focus the bulk of their energy internally on the people who are already there. Activist Boomers are attracted to organizations, especially churches, that take their message to the streets. Churches that hope to reach Boomers for Christ must get their hands dirty in ministry in their local communities. Begin by asking questions of civic leaders and reading local newspapers and then make a list of the needs and concerns in your immediate community. Share the findings with your people. Bear Valley Baptist Church in Denver took its entire congregation on a bus tour of the city to acquaint them firsthand with the city's needs. Ask people to pray about these needs and expect God to place burdens on people about becoming involved in finding answers. Look for four or five people who are interested in helping people solve their problems. Organize them into a task force and give them training and perhaps a little start-up capital but expect them to carry the weight and burden of making the ministry go.

Minister to Singles

According to *U.S. News and World Report,* fewer than 3 percent of the population lived alone in 1940. Today that number has risen to nearly 12 percent of the population—over 20 million! More than 50 percent of those living alone are women. While many singles are widows or widowers, there are increasing numbers of people who have chosen not to marry. And the number of singles who have been divorced will increase as people continue to follow the script of *Kramer vs Kramer* rather than *Ozzie and Harriet.*

Create multiple options in singles ministry. Typical college and career groups will flourish. But groups targeted to singles with children and midlife-never-married singles will enable your church to stand apart from others. Design social activities for parents without partners. Create classes that deal with the single lifestyle. Establish divorce recovery programs. Create a church atmosphere of acceptance for singles. Rethink the concept of a "family" church.

Use Sports and Retreats

When most of us think of camps we think of kids, hot dogs, ghost stories, name tags, sleeping bags, and bunks. But camp is no longer exclusively for kids. New camps specifically designed for adults are springing up everywhere, and old ones are retooling to meet the demands of adult audiences. For example, one and two week camps costing $1,000 or more offer training from tennis to golf to mountain climbing to sailing. Instead of hot dogs there are low-fat, high-energy diets for active people. In place of counselors, there are coaches and trainers. Along with fun, there is the desire to improve old skills and learn new ones. Many offer up to six hours each day of training and discussion on fitness and diet. A different slant to this is the living out of fantasies through camps such as Fantasy Baseball Camps where retired baseball players coach and play games with those who remember them. Then there are the members of the Cowboy Lawyers Association in Los Angeles who annually go to Colorado to live and work a few days on a western dude ranch. These "city slickers" live out their fantasies and reduce their stress all at the same time. These camps attract those mainly from ages twenty-five to fifty.

Likewise, a church should offer sports activities such as hiking, softball, basketball, and volleyball, as well as aerobics classes and other similar activities. Host a doubles tennis tournament with members inviting nonmembers to play with them. Or have your own sports camps. In addition, adult retreats can be sponsored with topics such as "Building Strong Relationships" or "Living Healthy and Happy."

Plant a Daughter Church

At least 100,000 new churches are needed in the United States to reach the Boomer Generation. New churches often bring a new style of ministry that is attractive to these middle-aged adults. They allow for the creation of new structures, are more open to new people, and create more vision and challenge than older churches. It has been estimated that there are only between 6,000 and 8,000 churches in the United States targeted directly to Boomers today—about 2.5 percent of all Protestant churches. That's only one church for every 9,500 Boomers.

Conclusion

In January 1990 Elmer Towns encouraged churches to retool to reach the Boomer Generation. His words still need to be taken seriously.

> Today they are junior executives or middle managers in business. When they become the primary influences in our country, culture will be molded according to their values and ideals. We must understand them now to reach them before it is too late. The coming Boomer Church can influence our culture but the congregations that ignore them will only be hibernating churches.[15]

The Boomer Generation has had tremendous impact on our society. The size of this generation has caused overcrowded classrooms and an overcrowded job market. As Boomers mature and their desires and tastes change, their needs will not be met as they were in the past, and their needs are very different from those of Builders when they were in midlife.

To effectively reach Boomers with the gospel, we need to correct our tunnel vision that has never allowed us to change our method of sharing the gospel. With a desire to reach Boomers and a willingness to tailor ministry to them, we can bring many to Christ in the years to come.

The Boomer Generation

Aliases	Yuppies (young, urban professionals) Oinks (one income, no kids) Dinks (double income, no kids) New Collars (information workers) Gold Collars (highly paid information workers) Postwar Babies Postwar Generation Vietnam Generation Sixties Generation Thirtysomethings & Fortysomethings Challengers Me Generation
Formative Years	1950s, 1960s, and 1970s
Formative Experiences	Cold War Television Economic affluence Education and technology Rock and Roll Civil Rights movement The new frontier Space race Assassinations Vietnam War and Kent State Energy crisis Watergate and Nixon resignation
Characteristics	Educated Media-oriented Independent Cause-oriented Fitness conscious

	Enjoy rock music Action-oriented Desire quality Question authority
Religious Characteristics	Committed to relationships Want to belong Supportive of people Want to live their faith Want experiences with faith Tolerant of differences
Boomer Ministry	Highlight purpose and vision Use celebrative worship Stress quality Streamline structure Offer multiple options Use small groups Restructure existing services Communicate visually Expand roles of women Focus on local ministry Offer short-term missions involvement
Common Needs and Concerns	Spiritual search Desire to return to traditional values Slower lifestyle Second career development Financial worries Reevaluating goals Midlife transitions Preparing for retirement Death of the American Dream
Reaching Unchurched Boomers	Emphasize family Develop bridge ministries Offer a seeker service

Stress lifestyle evangelism
Provide quality child care
Give opportunities for service
Welcome guests appropriately
Create opportunities for belonging
Minister to singles
Get involved in the community
Plant a daughter church

Part 3

The Buster Wave

7

Why Are They Called Busters?

The Simpsons television show is not known for saving people's lives. But in 1992 an episode was credited with helping to save the life of an eight-year-old boy. Karen Bencze of Auburn, Washington, informed Fox executives (producers of the sitcom) that her eight-year-old son was choking on a piece of orange when his ten-year-old brother performed the Heimlich maneuver on him, a technique he learned from a February episode of *The Simpsons.* After learning of the story, an executive producer of the series commented "It's great. Everyone at *The Simpsons* was shocked that anyone learned anything from our show. We'll try not to ever let that happen again."[1]

For some people *The Simpsons* picture the Buster Generation perfectly. To them, it is a wonder that the MTV Generation learns anything. Such a limited concept of the Buster

Generation is unfair. Like the Builders and Boomers before them, they compose a complex mix that cannot be generalized too narrowly.

The newest generation to be placed under the microscope, Busters go by several names. *Time* calls them the "Twentysomething Generation." *Fortune* has referred to them as "Yiffies," for young, individualistic, freedom-minded, and few. *Esquire* has labeled them the "Nowhere Generation." Most people simply call them Busters.

Broadly defined, Busters were born between 1965 and 1983 and represent 66 million Americans. They are called Busters because theirs is a smaller (bust) generation compared to their Boomer parents who make up the largest single generation in our history—76 million. Of course, 66 million Busters is not such a small number. It is the second largest generation to be born in the United States and honestly is not much of a bust. The term *bust* was actually given to only the first twelve years of the generation (1965–1976) when only 41 million babies were born. Compared to the 76 million Boomers this *was* a bust. Over the years the name has been used to include the entire generation.

Like their predecessors, Busters have been given numerous aliases in an attempt to characterize their distinctives. Names such as Post-Boomers (Posties), Echo Boom, and Baby Boomlet link them directly to their Boomer parents' generation. Twentysomethings points understandably to their primary age group while Tweens refers to younger Busters on the verge of being teenagers. The 13ers name recognizes them as the thirteenth generation since America's founding fathers. Generation X, a name taken from Douglas Coupland's 1991 novel, is becoming popular. It represents the unknown. We don't know what will be the ultimate identity of this generation. Many possibilities exist.

Busters, of course, are the children of the Boomers. Born between 1965 and 1983 they are now between the ages of twelve and thirty. Like the generations before them, Busters are not a homogeneous whole but may be divided into two distinct groups: the Bust and the Boomlet.

The Bust

Born between 1965 and 1976, Baby Busters are those between the ages of nineteen and thirty and represent 41 million people. Most of the studies of Busters have been made on this group because the second half has been too young to have developed a clear identity.

Influential Members of the Baby Bust

Troy Aikman, 29
Lisa Bonet, 28
Steffi Graf, 26
Ken Griffey Jr., 26
Janet Jackson, 29
LL Cool J, 27
Lisa Marie Presley, 27
Mary Lou Retton, 27
Gabriela Sabatini, 25
Brooke Shields, 30
Todd Stottlemyre, 30
Debbie Thomas, 28
Malcolm Jamal Warner, 25

Ages as of 1995

The Boomlet

Many Boomers married later in life or, if they got married at a young age, did not have children until their careers were established. The result has been a Baby Boomlet (sometimes referred to as an Echo Boom, although this name is being used more for those now under twelve years old). This second phase of births comprises the last seven years of the Buster Generation (1977–1983). Total head count of Boomlet babies is roughly 25 million. They are twelve to eighteen years old today. Although Generation X has expanded to include the entire Buster Generation, it specifically represents this younger teenager Boomlet.

Influential Members of the Baby Boomlet

Macaulay Culkin, 15	Joey Lawrence, 17
Bicole Dubuc, 17	Fred Savage, 17
Eddie Furlong, 18	Jodie Sweetin, 13
Balthazar Getty, 18	Elijah Wood, 14
Chelsea Hertford, 14	*Ages as of 1995*

Researchers seeking to characterize the Buster Generation have often made two mistakes. First, they think this generation is extremely cynical. Second, they believe it is only a younger version of the Boomers. Both, of course, are not correct. Busters have had a bad rap. Calling them Generation X and portraying all of them as a whining group of cynical youth is as inaccurate as calling all Boomers hippies. Likewise, assuming they are small versions of the Boomers misses the nuances that make them different from their Boomer parents. Like all generations, they have experienced similar events that have shaped a general character, and this allows us to see them as a distinct group.

The Buster Generation is still young, of course, so it's difficult to say what will ultimately characterize this generation. The events and economic conditions of the eighties and nineties have had an impact on the Busters. The formative years will continue into the 2000s.

The development of the Busters as a generation is important to our nation, for by the year 2015, Busters will begin to take over leadership of the United States. It will take that long for two reasons: The Boomer Generation is blocking their way, and a generation normally doesn't take over until a majority of its members enter their forties.

Shaping the Busters

Life-shaping events are easier to define after a generation has grown older. Tracing a characteristic back to a probable cause seems more accurate than attempting to predict the future. A Chinese proverb declares, "To prophesy is difficult, especially with regards to the future."

Enough time has gone by for the Buster Generation (at least the older ones) to see some prime events that have affected their thinking and living. A generational mystique does appear to be developing, one that will mature, to be sure, but one that can be identified at least in its initial phases.

Roe v. Wade

Roe v. Wade was a decision by the United States Supreme Court in 1973 concerning a woman's right to an abortion. The Court determined that a state could not restrict abortion during the first three months but could regulate abortions during the second trimester to protect a woman's health. During the final trimester states are allowed to prohibit abortions unless the pregnancy endangers the woman's health. One of the most controversial Supreme Court decisions of all time, it has been challenged and modified, but remains in place.

Since the oldest Buster was only eight years old at the time of *Roe v. Wade,* none of them will remember it directly. It has been a life-shaping event for their generation, however, since it has limited their birth rate dramatically. There is little doubt that the Buster Generation might have outstripped the Boomer Generation in size if babies had been born rather than aborted.[2]

High Technology

Growth of technology has increased dramatically during the Buster years. As an example, between 1946 and 1960 the number of computers grew from 1 to 10,000. From 1960 to 1980 to 10 million. By the year 2000 there will be over 80 million computers in the United States alone. The number of components that can be programmed into a computer chip is doubling every eighteen months.[3] Today it is a rare business, church, and even home that is without a computer. Busters are very comfortable with computers. In contrast, the Builder Generation grew up writing and using manual typewriters. Boomers started with manual typewriters and moved up to IBM Selectrics. The youngest of the Busters have never used a typewriter but usually are computer literate.

Video Games and Television

The popularity of video games is enormous. Atari founder Nathan Bushnell introduced the first video game in 1972. "Pong," a simple tennis game, sold over 6,000 units its first year. Atari's all-time top seller came in 1989 when "Super Mario Brothers 3" sold more than 7 million units in the first year. More recently their "Mortal Combat" game sold nearly 4 million in its first six months of release. The video game market grew so rapidly during the 1980s that in 1992 a search was made to determine the largest installed base of chip-driven devices in U.S. homes. Surprisingly it was not found to be IBM or Macintosh computers or even chip-driven appliances but 48.8 million Nintendos! The rapid-fire image changes in almost all video games mean that Busters who play them have had to develop visual acuity and the ability to respond quickly.

In the past two decades there has been a tremendous change in what is available to watch on television. With hundreds of cable stations to choose from, viewers have endless variety. There seem to be fewer restrictions on program content today, and violence and immorality are continuous fare. MTV, a network that appeals to young people through its often explicit music videos and its counterculture programming, is estimated to reach 20 million twelve- to twenty-five-year-olds.

Our technology today has made it possible for events to be televised as they happen. This has meant that people can watch crises anywhere in the world as they develop. A moment-by-moment account of Desert Storm, the assassination attempt of Ronald Reagan in 1981, or O. J. Simpson's slow drive on the Los Angeles freeway to give himself up to the police certainly have had an impact on Buster viewers. In 1979 when Iran took American hostages and held them for 441 days, television viewers saw images of the hooded victims over and over and were reminded nightly of the crisis. This detailed coverage of current events as they happen may make it difficult for Busters to separate fact from fiction.

The Challenger Disaster

On January 28, 1986, the space shuttle *Challenger* exploded moments after lifting off at Cape Canaveral, Florida. All crew members were killed, including the first private citizen astronaut, New Hampshire school teacher Christa McAuliffe. A later investigation discovered that a seal on a solid-fuel booster rocket was the prime cause of the explosion. The tragedy shook NASA and the world as the explosion took place on national television. The explosive images on television shook up many Busters, who were between the ages of three and twenty-one at the time. The *Challenger* disaster had an effect on older Busters that was similar to the impact that the assassinations of JFK and Dr. King had on their Boomer parents and that the attack on Pearl Harbor had on their Builder grandparents.

Berlin Wall Dismantled

East Germany built the Berlin Wall in 1961 as a barrier to stop the exodus of refugees from Communist East Germany to West Germany. Originally it was a barbed-wire fence but was later replaced by a five-foot-high cement block wall topped with barbed wire and broken glass. East German soldiers had orders to kill anyone trying to scale the wall.

In November 1989 a surprise move in the wake of a citizens' revolt led to the opening of traffic between East and West Germany and the eventual dismantling of the wall in 1989 and 1990. As the wall was torn down it was a symbol of the dramatic dismantling of Communism in other parts of the world. With the Cold War over, Busters gained hope that the world will be a safer place.

Peer Groups

As generations grow up certain institutions shape them into adults. For Builders the strongest influences were family, school, church, and the military. It was within these social institutions that they learned to think, act, and be adults. By the time the Boomers came along some of these socializing institutions began to lose their influence. Television and college began to have impact. Once again socializing institutions have changed and the Busters are learning about life (being socialized) through their peer groups and in the workplace. Often supervision in the workplace is by people not much older than themselves. They are making many decisions without adult supervision. Many Busters who have faced life in fractured, dysfunctional families have often resorted to their peers for support. Parafamilies such as gangs, sports teams, and clubs are helping shape them into adults. Many are opting to work before going to college. Coworkers become important to their developing adulthood.

Music

"I Want to Hold Your Hand" was the first Beatles song to hit the *Billboard* charts in the United States in January 1964. Listening to that tune today certainly shows that times have changed. Today's music portrays few illusions about life and love. It may not be more cynical than that of some thirty years ago, but it is less restrained in a culture where almost anything is allowed to be said or sung about. Punk rock, heavy metal, and gangsta rap are all types of this new unrestrained music.

Variable Economy

Busters may be inheriting a third-generation rags-to-riches story. Their Builder grandparents rode a developing economy by sacrificing, working hard, and saving. Their Boomer parents have lived through a strong economy, spending the wealth that had accrued. Depending on future turns of the economy, there may be little left for Busters. They are coming of age in a time of limited resources. They are facing a much weaker economy, which makes it more difficult to buy a home, pay off a mortgage, even find a job. During their life span the percentage of college students pursuing degrees in literature, history, and foreign languages has dropped while one major has increased dramatically—business. Busters are interested in business because it offers the best hope for careers that will be financially profitable. Busters must be careful to choose a career in a field that will need workers when they are ready to enter the workforce.

Persian Gulf War

On January 15, 1991, when Iraq failed to withdraw its troops from Kuwait, Operation Desert Storm began. U.S. and coalition forces attacked Saddam Hussein's army to force their withdrawal. A prolonged air attack and four days of ground combat were all that was needed to defeat Hussein's army. An estimated 100,000 Iraqi soldiers died in the battle with allied losses totaling less than 200.

The Gulf War was different from the Vietnam War in several ways. It was superbly planned and executed. It was short and cost few lives. It was sanctioned by Congress. It was supported by the American public. It was a war we won. Among Busters, this created a positive feeling about the United States and our armed forces.

AIDS

When basketball star Magic Johnson retired from basketball in 1991 due to being HIV positive, publicity about the AIDS epidemic rose sharply. AIDS (Acquired Immune Deficiency Syndrome), a disease of the immune system, is caused by a virus known as HIV (human immunodeficiency virus). First recognized in 1981, AIDS has since risen to epidemic proportions in the world. Originally found primarily in gay men in urban areas, it has now spread to heterosexual groups throughout the population. It has become a social and political issue as well as a health issue. In the United States more litigation cases have arisen as a result of AIDS than any other disease. The World Health Organization estimates that by the year 2000 more than 40 million people will be infected worldwide.

The effect of the AIDS epidemic on Busters is staggering. They are part of a culture where sex before marriage with multiple partners is accepted and expected, but if they indulge in sex, they know they may get AIDS and die. Never before has a generation had to be so aware of their own mortality.

Clinton Administration

Young Bill Clinton's excitement about meeting President Kennedy so inspired him that he decided he wanted to become president himself. His excitement was felt by most Boomers who saw the youthfulness of Kennedy, his wife, and family as a sign of hope for the future. Camelot was real, if only for a short while, in the hearts and spirits of the Boomers. It was real enough that Boomers volunteered for the Peace Corps and invested untold hours in helping less fortunate people in other countries as well as their own.

It is way too early to tell, but it is possible that the administration of President Bill Clinton will have a similar effect on the minds and spirits of Busters. The twenty-two-year age gap between him and former president George Bush was striking enough to make people take notice. Only John F. Kennedy entered the presidency with a larger age difference. He was twenty-seven years younger than outgoing President Dwight D. Eisenhower. If President Clinton can grow into the presidency and lead with honor and conviction, he may well inspire the Busters to greater works in the years ahead.

Buster Concerns and Characteristics

Members of the Bust Generation take their identity as much from what they are not as from what they are. They are not the Boomers, although the line separating them from the Trailing-Edge Boomers is a thin one.

It is impossible to give characteristics of the average Buster, save to say he or she is young and just really getting started in life. There are, however, some dominant themes that seem to characterize various segments of this generation and may be helpful in designing ministry to reach this new generation.

Freedom

Many Busters reject the workaholism often needed to acquire money and titles and to climb the career ladder. They do not expect to make personal sacrifices for the company, and they expect personal satisfaction from their jobs. To them, other interests are as important as work. Flexibility, work-free weekends, and short-term tasks with measurable results are expected.

Sixties Nostalgia

Busters flock to see Paul McCartney, the Who, and the Beach Boys. As with generations before them they hear about former times and wish they had lived then. The sixties is the era that attracts many Busters. It is far enough removed that the fighting and dying for causes can seem exciting and the life of a hippie romantic. Many Busters like sixties artifacts, such as peace signs.

The most frequently mentioned role model for all Busters is Michael Jordan. After him come people from the past: John F. Kennedy, Elvis Presley, James Dean, and Martin Luther King.

Issues of Survival

National and global issues such as world hunger, homelessness, AIDS, the federal deficit, poverty, and pollution are so large and complex that most people feel helpless to do anything about them. Busters seem to have no illusions about solving these problems, so they tend to focus on issues closer to home where they can see results. Fifty percent of Busters are environmentally conscious and are drawn to groups that have a well-focused message, choose specific targets, and get things accomplished quickly.

Because of problems such as pollution, poverty, AIDS, and the safe disposal of nuclear waste, Busters are very aware that the quality of life on this planet may drastically decline during their lifetime. The accidents at nuclear power plants at Three Mile Island in Pennsylvania and at Chernobyl have forced Busters to put survival goals above self-actualization goals.

Teenage Busters are also murdered twice as often as teenagers were in the sixties—roughly 2,000 were killed in 1988. Busters must deal with the stress of living in an increasingly dangerous world.[4]

Feeling Neglected

More than 40 percent of Busters are children of divorce. They were and are latchkey kids, which may mean they are neglected by parents who have been too occupied with their careers and personal freedom to pay much attention to them. Forty to 50 percent of teen Busters live in single-parent homes, usually headed by working mothers. Busters are twice as likely to come from broken homes as their Boomer parents and three times as likely as their Builder grandparents.[5] Often Busters are lonely. The things that teenagers plug into are marvels of communication, but these things isolate teens. Walkmans, computers, VCRs, and T.V.s are all causing teens to spend more time alone in their rooms.

Willing to Work

Seventy-five percent of part-time workers are under twenty years old. Between 1981 and 1989 the percentage of sixteen- to seventeen-year-olds working grew from 35.5 percent to 37.6 percent. Busters work for the same reasons youth have always worked—for extra spending money, to buy a car, to pay their way through college. Today many are choosing to work because they question the value of a college education. Most of the jobs open to them, however, are low-skilled and low-paying and thus are a negative introduction to the world of work.

The pool of entry-level workers sixteen to twenty-four has been shrinking 500,000 a year through 1995. Already companies like McDonald's have started programs to recruit workers from older generations. Talented Busters will move into entry-level jobs with no difficulty, but it may be difficult for them to reach higher levels in the job market. For several years, Boomers will block their way to advancement.

Boomer Values Rejected

Having observed what divorce, career climbing, and drug abuse have done to their Boomer parents, Busters are rejecting many of their parents' values and lifestyles. Forced to grow up too quickly, some of them have even had to "parent" their own parents. They appear to be more conservative and hold more traditional values. They hope to someday be happily married. Many, however, lack relational skills due to the broken and dysfunctional homes in which they are growing up.

Practical Education

Busters want an education that will help them get a job. The high cost of a college education and the competition for good jobs have forced Busters to be very practical about their education. Styles of learning have changed too. Builders were audio learners, willing to sit and listen to lectures. Boomers were visual learners, influenced by television. Busters are also visual learners, but they learn through experience as well. Technically referred to as kinesthetic learners, they want not only to "see" the lesson but to "feel" it.

Growing up in a media-saturated society has instilled in Busters an expectation of immediate satisfaction. The rapid pacing of television and video games gives them the impression that life moves quickly, and they become easily bored when things move slowly. Having grown up in a world with few mundane schedules, Busters are finding it difficult to complete assignments and projects requiring sequential work. Verbal and writing skills have declined, and Busters are being characterized as oversensitive at best and lazy at worst.

Postponing Marriage

According to *Time,* 75 percent of young adults eighteen to twenty-four years old still live at home, the largest portion since the Great Depression.[6]

Fortune reports that of men twenty-five to twenty-nine years old, 46 percent have never married. Thirty percent of women in that age bracket have never married. In 1970, 19 percent of men in the same age bracket and 11 percent of women had not married.[7] Busters may be overly cautious about marriage if they've experienced the unhappiness of a broken home. They may also find that they can have satisfying relationships outside of marriage that don't require long-term commitments.

Conclusion

In some ways, Busters have lost out on many of the things their parents and grandparents enjoyed. The economic condition of our country, the threat of environmental problems, and the many broken homes have created an insecure and often hopeless generation. Like all generations before them, only the love of Christ can truly heal their hurts and redeem their lostness.

8

Busters and the Church

Suddenly it seems that everyone is talking about them—the Busters, or Generation X. Cover stories in *U.S. News & World Report* and *Business Week,* along with numerous feature stories in the *New York Times, USA Today, Christianity Today,* and countless new books are finally coming to terms with the Buster Generation.

Early secular writers appeared to write off this 13er Generation. Thirteen is a number we try to avoid. Elevators do not stop at the thirteenth floor, donut bakers do not count number thirteen (it's a baker's dozen), and who likes to go out on Friday the thirteenth? Busters have been dismissed as simply empty, boring, and uninspired by some, and as cynical and selfish by others.

Neither is true, of course. Busters are just young and they act young. But they will mature, just like their Boomer parents did. They will chill out like most generations have before them.

Influences on Religious Involvement

"God loves Busters and so do we" would make a good motto for churches during the next twenty years. The church of the 2020s and beyond will be led by Busters so it is vitally important that we understand and minister to them today. What can we expect as we seek to minister to this generation? Here are a few key insights for consideration.

Importance of Family

Because so many Busters are children of divorced and dysfunctional families, they value a true family atmosphere. Dual-income and workaholic parents often could not or did not take the time to build healthy family relationships with their Buster children. The result has led Busters to place a heavy emphasis on family. Bill Marvel and Melissa Morrison, writing in the *Dallas Morning News,* confirm that "Thirteeners will establish marriages that are far more stable and enduring than those of their oft-divorced parents. And . . . they will become extremely protective parents, seeking to shield their children from the harsh realities they experienced growing up."[1] Family to Busters is broadly defined to include practically anyone who will be their friend. Thus, a Sunday school class or small group for Busters becomes more than that. It actually becomes family, or their parafamily.

Local Causes

Compared to their parents, who when they were young thought they could change the world, Busters are idealists with a small *i.* Busters want to make a difference in the world, but the causes they support are small *c* causes. More pragmatic than the generations before them, they want to be able to see the results of their involvement. Causes close to home attract their interest far more than national or worldwide causes.

Shorter Attention Span

One criticism of Busters is that they are aliterate; that is, they know how to read but choose not to. They are the "sound bite" generation that has been raised on fast-paced television shows and video games. Advertisers discovered a long time ago that the way to hold the attention of Busters is to make ads short and full of action. When it comes to church, the slow pace of most services bores Busters. They may sit through them, all the time knowing they were designed for their parents, not for them. Busters lose interest quickly, and churches that hope to reach them must consider this seriously or there will be fewer Busters in the seats next Sunday.

Up-to-Date Options

Churches that reach Busters for Christ will have innovative services and will be on the cutting edge technologically and musically.

For Busters, video games, faxes, cellular phones, ATM cards, compact discs, and computers have always been around. A church that doesn't have computers and the latest in audio-video equipment will seem old-fashioned.

Busters respond to short, pointed dramas that are part of the worship service. Sermons or classes that are straight lectures will not cut it. Busters learn best through experience and visual images. They respond to sermons delivered close to the audience, rather than from behind a pulpit, removed from the crowd. Illustrations about real people alive today touch their hearts more than stories of people who died long ago in places they are not familiar with.

Busters also like choice. The large number of choices they have daily is mind-boggling. When Boomers were growing up, they had a choice of three major television channels, but Busters have hundreds of cable channels to choose from. Boomers had a few movie theaters in town, but Busters have a choice of thousands of videos that can be viewed right at home. Larger churches continue to attract a disproportionate number of Busters because they can offer a greater number of choices.

Busters have a variety of musical tastes. For some it's rap while for others it's heavy metal or classic rock or jazz. Many like several different styles. Most younger Busters like their music loud and fast with a good beat. Much of the music Busters enjoy today has musical and emotional depth. Songs are experiences they want to feel and lose themselves in. A church that wants to attract Busters must have music that conforms to their tastes.

Faith That Meets Needs

A hurting generation always looks for answers, and Busters are no different. Society and school have taught them that there are no absolutes, and yet they long for the solid answers that only personal faith can provide. An absence of good values, the frustration of isolation, and the emptiness of their lives are all leading many Busters on a spiritual search.

First, Busters want their own needs met. Busters are very pragmatic about their faith. They want a faith that works for them. While all generations have had their share of problems, this generation experiences more dysfunctions, abuses, and broken families than any before it. The lack of strong support networks or moral ethics has resulted in a problem-ridden generation. Thus they look for a church that will nurture them and give them practical resources to survive in a post-Christian culture.

Second, Busters also want to meet the real needs of other people. They expect churches to be concerned about and involved with the social, political, and environmental issues of their local communities.

Less Structure

Look underneath their somewhat cynical exterior, and you will find that Busters have soft not hard hearts. They long to be accepted for who they are and to know that they matter to God. The new currency of life is not money but T-I-M-E. For this younger generation, free time has become more valuable than money. Thus, they do not tend to work overtime or take work home at night. With all the activities and pastimes available to them, Busters are busier than their Boomer parents were at the same age.

With the many demands on the Buster's time, structured church activities are often not top priorities. This means that Busters will probably be at fewer church activities than their Boomer parents. But Busters enjoy unstructured activities and will respond to those who are willing to spend time with them. The best way to touch their hearts for Christ is to simply spend time doing things with them. Taking time to play basketball or a table game will do more to open their hearts to the gospel than will most church services.

Stress

Today's younger generation is stressed out. There are few carefree days for Busters. Drugs, AIDS, gangs, violence, and crime threaten their well-being. The huge expense of college and the shrinking job market make them pessimistic about their futures. And the moral choices that confront them daily keep them constantly on the alert. A *San Francisco Chronicle* poll conducted in 1993 found that six out of ten Busters feel life is harder for them than for their parents.

Twenty-five percent of Buster women say their lives are "very stressful." Three of ten think that all the good jobs have been taken. Older Busters see Boomers holding all the good jobs, and they figure they will have five to ten years at the end of their careers when these jobs will be available to them.[2] They need help dealing with the stress and not a religion that piles on more burdens. Their faith needs to answer the YBH factor—Yes, but how? A religion full of "oughts" and "shoulds" will be rejected for one that provides the "whats" and "hows."

According to Scripture, Jesus was a man acquainted with grief, but he came to offer us abundant life. Many Busters have experienced grief in their short lives. Many have had unhappy home lives, and some have experienced the death of friends through suicide, drugs, or AIDS. They look for faith that is uplifting and a religion that accommodates great dreams and makes room for laughter.

Ministering to Busters

Busters are beginning to make their voices heard. Perhaps a new name is appropriate for them—the Re-Generation.

The Re-Generation is tired of feeling disenfranchised, disconnected, and overshadowed. They are beginning to step forward and take command of their lives. Alert church leaders need to step forward themselves and reach out in ministry to this Re-Generation. Here are some ideas.

Define Vision

Busters tend to prefer churches that have a clear focus, a narrowly defined vision, and a commitment to accomplish their mission. A mission statement such as "to know Christ and make him known" may be too theoretical to be relevant to Busters. A pragmatic generation, Busters want to know exactly where and how such a mission will be carried out. How are we actually going to get to know Christ? To whom exactly is the church trying to make Christ known? Busters also need to see evidence that members are involved in ministries that accomplish their mission.

Update the Worship Service

Churches that have short, well-planned worship services seem to attract Busters. Very time-conscious, Busters want to get on to the next project or activity in their lives. They need to feel that the church values their time and does not ask them to attend a service that is too long and is poorly designed or conducted. They probably grew up thinking that church is boring. They are not bored by worship but by services that move slowly.

Music is important to most Busters, and the generation has varied tastes. If a church is trying to attract Busters, up-to-date music and a variety of styles should be included in the worship service. Buster members should be involved in the selection and performance of the music.

Busters expect those who conduct a church service to strive for excellence. This MTV Generation practically grew up with remote controls in their hands. If a T.V. show did not hold their attention, they switched channels. Though they can't do this during a worship service that doesn't meet their standards, they do feel free to "switch channels" and attend another church.

Focus on Local Issues

Busters tend to prefer churches that focus on local ministry rather than ministry in faraway places. In this they are like their Boomer parents. They will volunteer to tutor school children and feed the hungry at a local soup kitchen. They will minister to the homeless or elderly in their own community. But they are seldom inspired to work for a ministry that's far from them geographically or philosophically. One important issue that attracts their attention and involvement is the environment. Anything a church can do to help improve the environment in their community will likely gain the support of Busters.

Busters will give money to churches where they can see their investment is bringing results. They like to know that their money is changing the lives of real people. Interviewing during worship services people who have been touched with the ministry of your church lets Buster members hear the results of their investment. Using videos of interviews or short CNN-styled reports is a powerful way to demonstrate the results of ministry.

Challenge to Short-Term Service

Busters are likely to volunteer for short-term ministry activities. The general rule of thumb is "recruit for the short-term and renew for the long-term." As with young people of every generation, Busters resist long-term commitments. So the best approach is to start small. Busters do need discipling in this area, however, so they can learn to make longer commitments. Once they have experienced success in ministry, invite them to sign on for a slightly longer time period.

Disciple through Small Groups

Busters usually enjoy the interaction of small groups. They are still young and immature, and they need the encouragement and feedback of a few people they can trust. Leaders need to watch for those who have difficulty applying general concepts to their own lives. For example, they may need help in recognizing who in their lives is their neighbor whom they should love. Some will need specific, step-by-step instructions and accountability. A small group is the best place for this to take place.

Answer Questions

Busters often need to sort out the hurts in their lives. Churches can help them do this through practical messages, classes, and small groups. Church leaders, especially those who preach and teach, need to get to know Busters and identify their felt needs. One-on-one interviews and small group discussions are good ways to find out what they are thinking and where they are hurting. In general, they are concerned with anything dealing with relationships, being successful in life, and healing inner pain from their childhood years. In this they may not be very different from church members from other generations, but because they are young the problems they face every day—sexual immorality, pornography, child abuse, drug/alcohol abuse, sexually transmitted disease, divorce, AIDS—can seem overwhelming. They need honest answers to their questions so they know how to deal with these issues.

Develop Need-Based Ministry

The fastest growing ministries in the United States over the past five years have been support ministries. Support groups and classes on topics like divorce recovery, overcoming addictions, and surviving abuse attract a large number of participants. Even one-day workshops on topics such as these will usually be well attended. Busters will be attracted to churches through need-based ministries that deal with the hurts and issues they are facing.

Conclusion

It is critical that we begin to understand the driving forces in the lives of Busters. If we hope to minister to them in our church, we need to be, to paraphrase an advertising slogan, "just slightly ahead of our time."

9

Reaching Busters

Busters are experiencing the standard transitions of life. Their top concerns at this point of life include having a good marriage and family, choosing a career, doing well in school, being successful in work, having strong friendships, paying for college, seeing the country go downhill, making a lot of money, finding purpose and meaning in life, and staying healthy. These are basically the same issues that every generation has been concerned with at their age. Christ has the answer to their concerns, but they are not asking the question in quite the way that previous generations have. Being the least churched generation to come along, they are not looking to the church for discussion, let alone answers.

As a church strives to design a strategy to reach unchurched Busters it should keep the following five concepts in mind.

1. Physically, nothing captivates Busters more than sports and fitness. They watch sports, play games, exercise, and stay even more fit than their Boomer parents. This is as true of women as men. Buster women have been the first generation to participate to a large extent in competitive athletics while in high school. Most junior highs, high schools, and colleges now have both men and women in swimming, weight lifting, soccer, volleyball, basketball, and softball. Gymnasiums are sure to become as important for churches that want to reach out to Busters as their sanctuaries are.

2. *Relationally, nothing captivates Busters more than friends and family.* As I've said, friends are often the family of Busters. Even if their biological family lives apart from them, they will still have a sense of belonging and roots. They are like all of us in that they need to belong and be loved, and they need to know that they are loved and appreciated for who they are more than for what they do. Involvement with friends in family-styled activities like dinners, parties, and holiday celebrations appeals to them. Group discussions centered around topics that families might discuss over dinner—what happened at work or school, local or national events, plans for the future, the pastor's message—are popular.

3. *Mentally, nothing captivates Busters more than entertainment and music.* Over their brief history Busters as a group have seen more movies, plays, sports events, concerts, and television than any other generation. They like to be entertained.

4. *Socially, nothing captivates Busters more than improving the environment.* Oil spills, the burning of rain forests, and the dangers of nuclear waste are documented on television on a regular basis. The Busters have not only heard about these problems, but they have experienced them personally through the television screen. As school children and youth they have written reports on the protection of dolphins, owls, fish, and eagles. They realize the necessity of recycling. They fear that before they really have time to enjoy

it, our earth may be destroyed. So, to them, protection of the environment is critical.

5. Spiritually, nothing captivates Busters more than a search for serenity. Busters have been dazzled with the numbers and types of technological innovations developed during their first twenty-plus years. From computers to cellular phones to Game Boys, they have become accustomed to products that make life easier and/or entertain. However, Busters are finding that the fruits of technology can isolate people. They are seekers looking for truth and are open to churches that will show them how to go about their search.

Reaching Unchurched Busters

Clark Morphew, a writer for Knight-Ridder Newspapers, sums up the opportunity for churches who wish to reach unchurched Busters with the gospel. He advises, "Teach these people how to pray, meditate and relax and they will stick with you forever. Ignore their spiritual needs and they will drift away in search of serenity in all the wrong places."[1]

Keep in mind that a one-size-fits-all approach to ministry will not work with Busters. They are a diverse group, and successful ministry to them will depend greatly on the age group, social background, and even geographic location of your Busters. You will have to experiment to find the best activities for the Busters you are trying to reach. Be ready to try new approaches. Here are some tips for churches that seriously wish to reach Busters with the good news of Jesus Christ.

Become a Buster-Friendly Church

Looking at churches from the Busters' point of view, there are three styles of churches: Buster-centered, Buster-friendly, and Buster-hostile. A Buster-centered church greets Busters with an excited "Welcome, we've prepared this church just for you." A Buster-friendly church greets Busters with a friendly "We thought you might drop by. Come on in and enjoy yourself." A Buster-hostile church greets Busters with a disgruntled "What are you doing here?"

Not every church can or should be Buster-centered. That approach is for churches that feel called to target Busters exclusively. Every church should be a Buster-friendly church, however. Every church should prepare for and expect that Busters will drop by. Some churches will remain Buster-hostile and, if they are also Boomer-hostile, they will not be with us for too many more years.

Remember that unchurched Busters are already predisposed to not like church, so to be a Buster-friendly church you must begin to do the following:

- Play down titles and use first names.
- Eliminate churchy sounding words like *foyer, vestibule,* and *sanctuary* and replace them with common terms like *platform, auditorium,* and *lobby.*
- Provide excellent child-care facilities. You may find about 75 percent of your Busters are still unmarried, but the 25 percent or so that are married and have children will want superior facilities for their children.
- Explain everything you do so unchurched Busters will have some idea of what is going on.
- Use music like what they listen to in their cars and at home.
- Dress casually.
- Remodel the church so that it reflects contemporary colors, fabrics, and styles. Obviously, a church cannot remodel every year, but put in place a plan that allows for remodeling at least every five years so that unchurched people will not view your church as outdated.
- Install equipment that Busters expect, such as air-conditioning and computers.

- Do not call attention to Buster guests. Welcome them as a group, invite them to sit back and enjoy the service, and direct them to a welcome center for further information and refreshments.

Value Busters

Busters have found very little in our world that is directed specifically to them as a group. Their Boomer parents may have ignored them as they pursued careers. Churches have ignored them, preferring to minister to the Builder Generation. As a result, many unchurched Busters feel lonely and neglected and are looking for some person, group, or institution that will love and value them. Churches that take time to understand Busters, and then minister to them, will find Busters very responsive. This will involve such things as

- a worship service using their music
- sermons, seminars, and workshops that touch on the needs they are facing
- scheduling that allows for limited commitments
- support groups that help them heal their hurts
- opportunities for them to develop relationships
- an atmosphere that helps them experience their faith
- a dress code that is relaxed
- teaching that focuses on the basics of the Christian faith, avoiding Christian clichés
- programming for singles, young couples, and families
- extending a welcome that overlooks nonconformity and allows for appropriate tolerance in all of life's arenas

Start a Seeker Service

Begin a worship service targeted to Busters who may be seeking the Lord or at least answers to their spiritual needs. Be sure to

- Choose the best time. Busters typically like a church service that starts between 9:00 and 10:00 A.M. Some careful research will help you determine the best time to start in your particular area.
- Make a good first impression. Busters are unsure about churches in the first place. They will make a decision about your church within thirty seconds of entering the front door, so make that first thirty seconds good.
- Keep things relaxed. Eliminate any aspect of the service that is not absolutely necessary if it might place undue pressure on the Buster.
- Be positive. Help Busters see the joy in serving Christ.
- Use a response card. Never ask Busters to walk forward or stand up or raise their hand to indicate any personal decisions. Instead ask them to indicate a decision on a response card. You will get a better response and not alienate Busters already scared of church.

In addition you may want to

- Start a drama ministry. Drama allows you to remove barriers by drawing Busters into the theme of the message and raising questions that you will answer in your message. The actors should be close in age to the Busters in the audience. Drama is not always appreciated by the Builder Generation, but it works well with Busters because they are media-oriented. Even though a drama ministry can be effective, no drama is better than bad drama. Begin by performing one skit per month and then work up to a weekly one as the talent surfaces.
- Develop a video production team. If you are really bold you could start a CTN (Church Television Network) or a WTN (Worship Television Network) or an MTN (Ministry Television Network). Use video to produce

documentaries about people who have had their lives touched by Jesus and your church. Produce a ten-to-fifteen-minute introductory video about your church and the ministries you have to offer. Give every prospective Buster a copy. At the very least, put the words to your choruses on slides or transparencies. Whatever you do, pack up the hymnbooks and put them away.

Preach "How to" Messages

Busters are looking for messages that tell them how to be successful in life. Sermon titles such as "How to Raise a Happy Family" or "How to Develop Loving Relationships" will often draw many listeners. Before giving a message to Busters, you should be able to give the "take away" value in one statement. Doug Murren, senior pastor of Eastside Foursquare Church in Kirkland, Washington, which ministers primarily to Boomers, feels that he has about one minute to earn their ear for the next twenty to thirty minutes. If he has only one minute to capture the attention of Boomers, you have only about thirty seconds to get Busters interested in your message.

The messages you preach should relate to one of the following three areas: relationships, purpose in life, and healing emotional scars. Be real and approachable. Use honest and up-to-date illustrations that show how to find an answer or deal with a specific problem. Use the practical part of the message to lead into the spiritual part. For example, begin with human relationships and bridge into relationship with God. It seems easier to reach Busters through the heart rather than the head, through emotions rather than the mind.

Educators tell us that people have different learning styles. As is often true with young people, many Busters learn best experientially. As they participate in activities and get involved emotionally, they receive the most benefit from the teaching.

Leaders and teachers of small groups, classes, and seminars must take the Busters' learning style seriously. Creative teaching techniques that involve the learner in the process will produce better results and application than simple lecturing. While some lecture is needed in classes and seminars, teachers should always build in an experiential component. Pastors can involve the audience experientially in the messages with carefully chosen illustrations, rhetorical questions, and drama.

In all cases, remember that many Busters have had less church background and have less biblical knowledge than their Boomer parents or Builder grandparents. Much of what they hear in a sermon may be new to them. They may take longer to assimilate information and will respond with the YBH factor—"Yes, but how?"

Busters tend to be visual learners, rather than cognitive learners. When information is not presented in a visual form, it may take them longer to digest. Never assume Busters know how to put the message into practice. Tell them how to do it in precise practical terms. Every lecture, message, and presentation must include the exact steps for implementation or application.

Establish New Ministries

The churches that effectively reach and win unchurched Busters almost always do so by starting something new rather than modifying an existing program or ministry. Starting a new group, a new ministry, a new worship service, and in a lot of situations, a brand new church, is often needed to reach unchurched Busters.

Large group activities where Busters can get together in groups of fifteen to thirty people work well. Sports activities are good for this and also evening discussion groups.

Guest speakers with special expertise can be invited. For Busters who lack the people skills needed in small group settings, larger groups may be the answer. They provide a party atmosphere that Busters appreciate, especially if music is used.

Churches have used sports in the past as a form of fellowship for their church members. Sports and recreation are often successfully used to reach unchurched Busters. Find out what recreational activities are popular with Busters in your area and put together outings or teams to attract them. These activities can be for both men and women and might include volleyball, softball, basketball, aerobics, biking, golf, racquetball, mountain climbing, and hiking.

You may want to consider scheduling retreats for various groups of Busters. Youth leaders understand that one of the best places to reach teenagers for Christ is at a camp. When people are removed from their normal everyday environment, they begin to relax and think about issues that usually never cross their minds. It is in these relaxed camp settings that many youth find Christ.

A similar possibility exists when Busters are away for a retreat. A retreat will attract unchurched Busters if it is built around sports activities such as skiing, boating, or mountain climbing or if there is a special speaker on a topic of interest. Comfortable accommodations and good food should be provided. Be sure to treat your Buster guests as adults.

Provide Parafamily Structures

For many Busters, a Buster-friendly church may become closer to them than family. Developing parafamily structures such as small groups for singles, young marrieds, and single parents will often meet needs for support and advice.

Other parafamily structures include sports teams, worship teams, small informal gatherings, and task-oriented committees. Parafamily structures can be small—from two or three up to six or eight. If they're much larger, they often cease to function as a family structure, and there is not as much opportunity for personal attention.

Busters are often easily influenced by a caring adult. Studies made of youth from troubled homes who later made good in life have found that in almost all cases a caring adult figure was present as a constant in that kid's life. Divorce recovery workshops; discussion groups; counseling programs; retreats; and support groups for children of alcoholics, children from abusive homes, and children living in blended families, all facilitated by a loving adult, will reach the hearts of many Busters.

Teach Life Skills

It is in families that most people learn life skills such as how to manage money, care for others, discipline themselves, and manage their time. These skills are needed to get along well in life. The broken family and dysfunctional background of many Busters has left them with a lack of training in these traditional skills. Churches can meet these needs and reach out to unchurched Busters at the same time. Short, two- or three-hour seminars on topics such as "How to Get Along with Difficult People," "How to Make a Budget," and "How to Manage Your Time" will often attract Busters who are struggling in these areas. To get started you should survey unchurched Busters in your church's ministry area to discover their concerns. Then develop a short workshop and advertise it where they are sure to see the advertisement (not in the church program). During the workshop, don't preach at them. Give them an honest workshop on the topic advertised. Your goal is not to bring people to Christ through this type of workshop but to help them get to know and trust the people of your church and to help them feel comfortable coming to your church building.

Be Involved in the Community

If a church wishes to meet and reach the Busters of its community, it should become involved in community projects. Working together helps build trust between Christians and the Busters who get involved. Busters are often interested in projects having to do with kids from broken homes, homelessness, unemployment, and the environment. Your church might organize groups to paint the homes of elderly people or be big brothers and sisters, host a monthly birthday party, or provide tutoring or music lessons for needy children. Become involved in substance abuse meetings and recovery groups that are open to the community at large.

Stress Marriage and Family

Busters are more like their grandparents than their parents when it comes to the value they place on family. One 1990 poll showed that "64 percent of men and women aged 18–29 said they wanted to spend more time with their own children than their parents had spent with them."[2] Busters are often interested in how to make family relationships work. Provide classes, workshops, and retreats for training in marriage and family development. Sponsor family outings or special events about every six weeks.

Many Busters may have grown up in dysfunctional families and plan to do better by their own children, but Busters will still adopt many of the values and opinions of their parents. There is far more congruence than conflict between the views of Boomers and Busters. Many Busters need to learn the skill of conflict resolution, and for many the first conflict to resolve will be with their parents. While this cannot and should not be forced, it can be encouraged appropriately. When Busters see restored relationships among their peers and their families, this is a powerful testimony.

Communicate Your Vision

Communicate the purpose and vision of your church with concrete examples of what is meant. Since people tend to lose sight of a vision within about two weeks, tell them over and over in various ways and with different examples. As a rule of thumb mention the direction of your church at least biweekly and tie it directly to a practical result or ministry that you are involved with at the present. Communicate effectively by using video, newsletters, cards, and drama.

Offer Time and Space

Busters are seekers on a spiritual pilgrimage, and their pilgrimage is likely to last longer than those of earlier generations. This is true for several reasons. First, they are the first post-Christian generation, so many of them lack the foundation of a Judeo-Christian upbringing. There's a lot of groundwork that must be laid before they can make a commitment to Christ. Second, they carry many hurts that will need healing before they can move on to another phase of their lives. Third, they learn by experimenting, and it takes time to experiment. Fourth, since they have not grown up in the church, they are predisposed to think the church is irrelevant. Patience, flexibility, and love are the ingredients needed to build a ministry to this unchurched generation.

Conclusion

Most researchers agree that Busters are a hurting generation. Pastor Dieter Zander planted NewSong church in

Southern California in order to reach the emerging Buster Generation. Within six years, NewSong grew to more than 1,200 worshipers with an average age of twenty-six. Zander's study and experience with Busters confirmed that the Busters' main needs are relationships, purpose in life, and personal healing.

Many Busters are already a generation removed from the church. They do not understand it and may think it is irrelevant. Yet some churches are reaching out to unchurched Busters and finding success in touching their hearts for Christ. These churches tend to focus on the needs and pain of Busters and thereby build bridges to them to share the gospel of Jesus Christ. Churches that heal hurts and build bridges will touch the lives of Busters.

The Buster Generation

Aliases	Yiffies (young, individualistic, freedom-minded, and few) 13ers (13th generation from the founding fathers) Twentysomethings Tweens (young Busters on the verge of being teenagers) Posties (Post-Boomer generation) Generation X Echo Boom Baby Boomlet The Reagan Generation
Formative Years	1980s, 1990s, and 2000s
Formative Experiences	*Roe v. Wade* High technology Video games and television The *Challenger* disaster

	Berlin Wall dismantled Peer groups and work Music, music, music Variable economy Persian Gulf War AIDS Clinton administration
Concerns and Characteristics	Freedom Sixties nostalgia Community causes Feel neglected and lonely Willing to work Reject Boomer values Want practical education Postpone marriage
Religious Involvement	Committed to family Local causes Shorter attention span Want up-to-date options Want faith that meets needs Want less structure Need to relieve stress
Buster Ministry	Define vision Update worship service Focus on local issues Short-term service Use small groups Answer questions Develop need-based ministries
Common Needs and Interests	Sports and fitness Friends and family Entertainment and music

	Improving the environment Search for serenity
Reaching Unchurched Busters	Become Buster-friendly Value Busters Start a seeker service Preach "how-to" messages Establish new ministries Provide parafamily structures Teach life skills Be involved in the community Host large group activities Schedule retreats Stress marriage and family Communicate your vision Offer time and space

Part 4

Riding the Waves of Change

10

Blending Generations

A recent article in the real estate section of a local newspaper highlighted a new home development, which was built for multiple-generation families. Home builders and architects have become aware that families are once again living together as multigenerational units. Throughout history it has been common for multigenerational families to live close together, if not actually under the same roof.

After World War II the development of the suburbs, freeways, and the resulting mobility of people broke geographic generational ties. Families began to live in smaller nuclear units rather than in extended family units. Now, towards the end of the twentieth century, families are finding it economically advantageous for several generations to pool their resources and live together.

The residences being advertised in the newspaper article were in Las Vegas, but a similar trend is taking place in other metropolitan areas of the United States. The architect who designed the new multigenerational homes for the Las Vegas development says, "Our consumer research for this house shows that today's families require flexible floor plans that accommodate multiple generations." He continues, "We designed [the homes] for a moderately affluent, multigenerational family—a mother, father, two children and live-in grandparent. The home breaks into separate functional areas—shared family spaces as well as private retreats for each generation."[1]

This blending of generations in living arrangements is something that needs to be followed in our church ministries. Some churches today specifically target Boomers or Busters, but for most existing, traditional churches this kind of narrow focus is not possible. Most pastors and church leaders know that they must work with all generations in the same church without ignoring any of them.

One popular approach used by some churches is to attempt a blend of the traditional and the contemporary in hopes of pleasing all generations enough so that they remain in the church. Before discussing blending, we need to clearly understand that the three generational divisions broadly discussed in the first three parts of this book are not to be

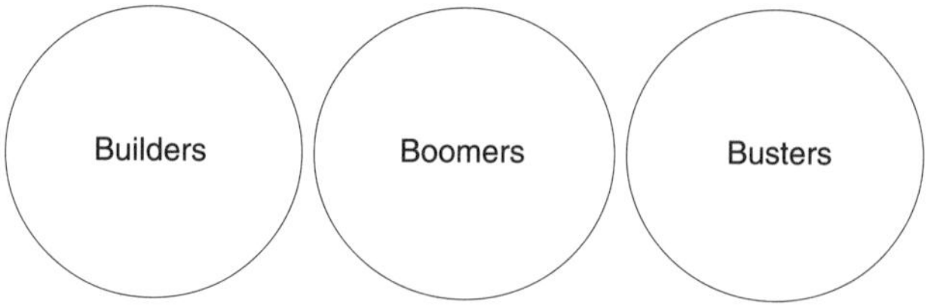

Figure 1

rigidly held. Figure 1 illustrates how a strict view of each generation might look. Perceived in this manner, we might get the idea that every person in each generation thinks exactly the same. Of course this is not true. The general characteristics of each generation are strictly true of only about three-fourths of each generation.

A wise pastor once noted, "There are old young people and young old people." Similarly, there are overlapping attitudes and characteristics among every generation that go beyond age or the particular generation in which an individual is born. Some Boomers will be very traditional in their outlook on church and ministry, while some Builders will enjoy the excitement of contemporary music and worship. Figure 2 illustrates a more accurate picture of the three generations. There is overlap of the generations at both ends. Since people born at the beginning or end of each generation grow up during a transition from one generation to

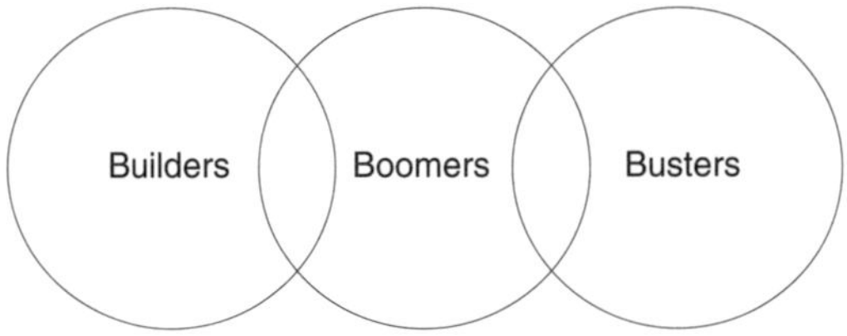

Figure 2

another, they feel strong pulls both ways and may go in either direction. It is very common to find some older Boomers who identify more with the Builders than with their own generation. Likewise, there will be some Busters who identify more with Boomers, and the opposite is also true.

We find that relationships between generations are even more complex. There are traditionalists in every generation who may identify with those a generation removed. Builders

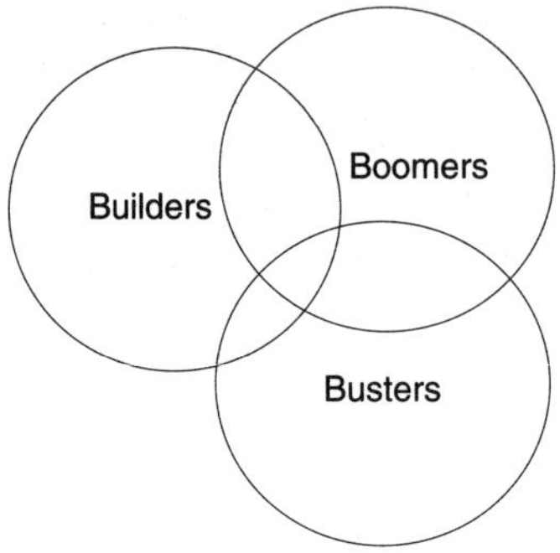

Figure 3

who once argued with their Boomer children over the Beatles' music may today accept the more aggressive music of their Buster grandchildren. And some Busters may feel very comfortable in their grandparents' church. There is less overlap between Builders and Busters and more overlap between Boomers and Busters, which is reflected in figure 3.

What Is Blending?

When church leaders talk about blending they usually are thinking of the worship service. No other ministry in a church reflects the values and philosophy of a church as clearly or as publicly. Worship is the one ministry in a church where all the members come and participate. The need for blending in other areas of ministry, such as Sunday school, is not as critical since the individual classes allow each generation the opportunity to do ministry in their own unique manner.

From a technical viewpoint, blending is the combining of two or more differing philosophies of ministry. Usually the differing philosophies involved are called "traditional" and "contemporary."

An attempt at blending in the worship service usually takes one of two forms. In the first, the worship time is segmented into two evenly divided sessions. One session will include music in a traditional style while the other uses music in a contemporary style. One may use the organ and

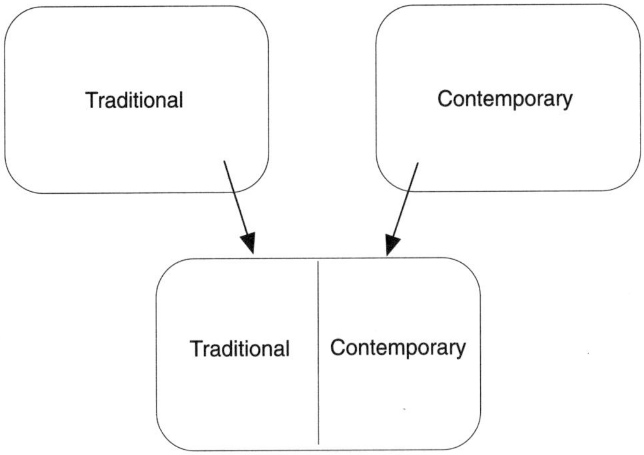

Figure 4

piano with hymns led by a song leader. In the other, a worship leader directs praise songs, accompanied by a small band. Although this option may meet the needs of all worshipers, the service may seem too choppy and fragmented. In addition, the generations tend to participate wholeheartedly only in the style they feel comfortable with, which reduces the volume and dynamic feel so important to a positive worship service (see figure 4).

A second approach to blending attempts to develop an entirely new style for worship, as opposed to using both traditional and contemporary styles as described above. The usual approach is to soften the contemporary music and speed up the traditional music so that the service becomes acceptably contemporary (see figure 5 on the following page).

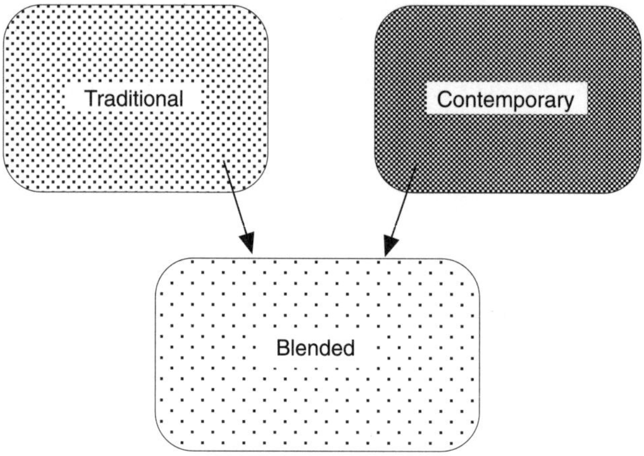

Figure 5

Most churches that wish to blend their worship services find that this second approach works best since it effectively weaves the two styles into a common, unified whole. Developing such a blended church usually takes some time, as illustrated by the following true story.

Faith Community Church was born during the church-planting boom of the early 1950s. Initially there was rapid growth, but following the resignation of the founding pastor the church plateaued. By its twenty-second anniversary the average member's age was over fifty. During this same period of time the local neighborhood gradually changed, attracting many Boomers due to the affordable housing. Faith found it was a Builder church unable to reach its Boomer community. With the calling of a young twenty-nine-year-old pastor, the church began to make some strategic changes to blend the Boomers with the Builders. Over a period of ten years several changes took place resulting in a blended church with an average age of under forty.

In the initial stage of change the large pulpit was replaced with a smaller one. The hard wooden pews were sold and replaced with moveable padded chairs. A new hymnal was purchased that contained some contemporary praise songs. Gradually, the congregation began to use the sanctuary as a multipurpose room. Creative use of the sanctuary allowed for gradual experimentation with different worship styles. For the evening service, the chairs were positioned at a different angle than used in the morning service. Various teaching techniques were tried in the evening, such as interviews, question-and-answer times, and panel discussions. Small groups were established, and new ministries directed to the needs of younger families were started. Today Faith is a totally blended congregation using a contemporary style of worship and music.

Nine Steps for Blending

The following are vital steps that should be taken by church leaders who desire to blend Builders, Boomers, and Busters into one church.[2]

1. Get senior pastor's support. It is often said that what is endorsed from the pulpit will succeed, and what is not will fail. The pastor must play the key role in planning, educating, and leading the church toward a blended ministry. For such a different emphasis to take place, the senior pastor must be committed to it and work to make it happen. No matter how strong the pressure, it is wise never to attempt to build a blended ministry without the senior pastor's full involvement.

Going beyond simple endorsement of the strategy, a pastor must be comfortable with and able to mesh two differing philosophies of ministry into a single new form. If the pastor's ministry has been geared to only one generation, he must be willing to communicate to a blended audience, find and use new illustrations, change his wardrobe (perhaps wearing a sweater and tie on Sunday morning), develop a relational style, adapt his vocabulary to be meaningful to all members, accept criticism, support the musicians and staff both publicly and privately, share creative leadership with a worship team, and patiently give the process time. A blended service that is well done is complex and difficult to do. It takes a lot of planning, and a pastor must be willing to prepare sermons and plan worship services two or three months in advance.

2. *Get support of lay leaders.* Lay leaders in the congregation must be willing to follow the pastor's lead. Their personal and group commitment to disciple making must cause them to see the needs and opportunities available in a blended church. They must team with the pastor in a strategic, long-term plan to bring the generations together.

A solid commitment to outreach and assimilation will undergird their willingness to try a blending approach to worship. Criticism will come from saints who feel that they are being neglected. As this occurs, the leaders' commitment to finding and keeping the lost *one* will need to outweigh the pressure to minister to the *ninety-and-nine* who are already in the church (see Luke 15:4–7).

3. *Help the congregation see the opportunities and needs.* Existing congregations must develop a desire to reach Busters and Boomers. Church leaders should plan to spend a minimum of six to twelve months creating such a consciousness before many changes or new strategies are implemented. Take the time to build a solid biblical foundation, share the vision for a new style of ministry, listen to people's concerns, adjust the proposed strategy, and pray.

4. *Stress biblical concepts of love and acceptance. Diversity* and *variety* are two words that characterize the Boomer and Buster Generations. The divergent views, desires, and expectations of Builders, Boomers, and Busters will require acceptance and love. Sermons, classes, and small groups should focus on these divergent ideas during the blending period.

In particular, stress the "one another" commands found in the New Testament and structure opportunities for people from different generations to practice them in small group settings.

5. *Establish an alternate worship service or a new class in which blending can be practiced.* It could be an evening worship service, a Sunday school class, or a small group. If this is not possible, an occasional praise or celebration service where new styles of music can be introduced will gradually introduce the congregation to blending. The gradual approach will help people to accept new ideas, which can eventually be introduced on a regular basis.

The model service ought to reflect a balance of traditional and contemporary styles in music, participation, relationships, and dialogue. It works best if the organization, transitions, feel, and flow of the new blended service are well thought out and developed before you go public with the service.

6. *Educate the generations so they understand each other.* A common term used in the 1960s to describe the gulf between Builders and Boomers was "generation gap." Generation gaps had been relatively unknown in earlier times since the slowness of change created very little difference in viewpoints between past generations. The rapid pace of change since 1950 has made generation gaps real.

How each generation views the gap is different. Younger generations tend to focus on the intrinsic differences in values, and older generations tend to focus on the immaturity seen in the personal habits and styles of the younger. Teaching from the pulpit must be geared to help each group see the value of the other. Key areas of concern are music, expression of worship, relational values, institutional values, and commitment levels. Everyone who speaks from the platform should take great care to affirm and hold up each generation. In no case should a generation ever be criticized publicly. The congregation gets its cues from its leaders. What is said and done during the worship service will flow down into the rest of the church.

Meet with Sunday school classes and small groups to teach about the strengths and values of each generation. These smaller forums allow for questions and answers as well as providing a safe place for people to vent their frustrations. By using these smaller forums, you will circumvent the possibility of an explosion of frustration in a larger setting, which may damage the entire body. As needed, meet with individuals over breakfast or lunch to hear their concerns.

In many cases the use of outside speakers or church consultants can prove to be a powerful change motivator. Being from the outside, they have several advantages such as being able to say things that could not be said by a member of the church family, having a more objective outlook, and being viewed as an expert on the issue.

7. Foster common ground experiences. Generations tend to drift apart in churches. The natural process of scheduling classes, small groups, and activities around life stages tends to segregate the generations and limit their communication. The offering of age-graded activities is proper, and there is no need to blend every ministry in a church. It does help generations to understand and love each other, however, when they spend time together. Leading up to and during the initial stages of developing a blended worship service, it is wise for church leaders to provide common ground experiences for the generations.

A new-members class could introduce people to the values, goals, and history of all three generations. A parenting class might be attended by a mix of Boomers, Busters, and Builders. The Builders could share the struggles they went through raising young children and answer questions. Since many Busters, in particular, came from homes where parenting skills were not well modeled, this could provide a solid opportunity to build bridges between the generations. An effort should be made to make small groups intergenerational. Many Builders, Boomers, and Busters enjoy being around people of the other generations.

8. Organize a new-members task force. The responsibility of this task force would be to help new people develop several friends in the church, find a place to serve, and identify a class or group where they would feel comfortable. Representatives from each generation should serve on the task force. It is crucial that the task force include people who are recent newcomers to the church (within one or two years) so they remember what it was like to have been a new member. They can help new people understand and fit into the existing church structure with a minimum of frustration.

9. *Encourage Boomers and Busters to take leadership.* If Builders have been the main leaders of your church, qualified Boomers and Busters must gradually be allowed and encouraged to assume key positions of leadership throughout the church structure. These would include the worship team, new-members committee, the worship committee, the music committee, the small group committee, the activities (social/sports) committee, as well as regular boards and committees, such as elders, deacons, or trustees.

It is crucial that the worship team be intergenerational. The leaders who are seen on the platform influence the people who will attend the service. When people come to a church one of the first things they do is look around to find people like themselves. The people on the platform communicate a tacit message about who attends the church. In a blended worship service care must be taken to have people of all ages up front. If the members of the worship team on the platform are only from the Builder Generation, then the service will naturally attract Builders but not Boomers and Busters. If a church wishes to attract and hold Busters, then it must have Busters on the platform. If the senior pastor comes from the Builder Generation, then it is even more important that Boomers and Busters be visibly present before the congregation.

Some Cautions

A well conceived and executed worship service of any type is more difficult to pull off than it looks to most people. And a blended service can be the most difficult of all. Remember that a blended worship service is likely to be a temporary worship form on the journey to a new form that is just right for your congregation. The exact mix or blend of worship elements may change several times on the journey. A blended worship tends to discourage those who want only one type of service. These people may become disheartened and move to other churches that offer what they want. Be aware that blended services may 1) be difficult to lead, 2) result in disruption, and 3) lose a sense of direction.

Blending at its best is transitional. In truth, blending is not the destination but the journey, and where worship services end up stylistically may not be known for many years. Some keen observers of churches feel that blending will only lead to a fully contemporary worship service. Others sense that we are in the dynamic process of creating an entirely new form of worship, which will only be evident over time.

Until that new form of worship is developed, blending generational styles in one service has proved a practical way to go. At the least, blending allows a church to

- demonstrate the unity of the church
- meet different needs
- provide diverse ministry opportunities
- honor the past and the future
- give people time to change

Conclusion

Vital, growing churches in the next decade will be those that can successfully reach, win, and keep the Boomer and Buster Generations. For this to happen in existing churches, leaders need to make bold, long-term plans for blending Builders, Boomers, and Busters into a unified church. Of course, there are risks involved in attempting a blend, but the call of Christ to make disciples makes the risks worthwhile.

11

Undercurrents of Discontent

As leaders who are trying to navigate through the waves of generational change in our churches, we will find ourselves pulled in several different directions by the undercurrents of discontent among our members. Being aware of where these undercurrents are and understanding a little bit of what causes them will help us ride safely over the waters of change.

Developing a ministry that meets the needs of the three generations may create several disruptive undercurrents. The following are the main ones faced by most churches when the generations collide.

Conflict over Worship Styles

The most visible ministry in which generational conflict shows up is the worship service. Disagreements over worship are so common that some pastors jokingly note that when Satan fell from heaven he landed in the choir loft and has been making trouble in the music and worship of the church ever since.

While not every member of each generation sees things the same way, essentially the areas of difficulty are as follows:

- Pace of the service. Builders like worship services to move along slowly and predictably. Boomers like worship to move at a fast clip, and Busters want it to move even quicker. Both Boomers and Busters look for some variety and spontaneity.
- Brightness of the lighting. Builders prefer softer lighting as it gives more of a worshipful feeling. Boomers and Busters look for a brighter lighting so they can see people well.
- Loudness of sound. Builders appreciate being able to hear well but dislike sound that blasts. Boomers and Busters want the sound loud so they can feel it.
- Length of service. Builders have a longer attention span and thus are willing to sit through longer services. The attention span of Boomers and Busters is shorter. They prefer a service that is no longer than seventy-five minutes.
- Formality of service. Builders expect a certain level of formality and decorum whereas Boomers and Busters like things to be flexible and casual.
- Feel of the service. Builders look for a worship service that is quiet and reverent. Boomers and Busters want an upbeat celebration time.
- Participation in the service. Builders tend to watch and enjoy while Boomers and Busters who grew up in church like to participate. Unchurched Boomers and Busters want to be entertained.

- Type of music. Builders love the hymnal and the familiar songs of the faith. They like their music to be slowly paced and reverent. Boomers and Busters like to "sing a new song" to the Lord. They like their music to be upbeat and loud.

Clash over Sermon Form

Sermons may be characterized as either vertical or horizontal. Vertical sermons stress the exposition of the Bible and tend to be oriented to touching people's minds. Builders like to nod in agreement with the truth they already know. They love to hear the old, old story over and over.

Horizontal sermons stress the practical application of the Bible and tend to be oriented to touching people's hearts. Boomers and Busters appreciate the old, old story, but they want to be challenged with what they do not already know. "You touched my heart" is their idea of a good message.

The Builder Generation usually likes a traditional message. Some like an in-depth Bible sermon and others prefer a more evangelistic message.

Boomers and Busters usually prefer a message with life application. They long for some practical word that will help them get through the week. As one person put it, "I'm more concerned about getting through Monday morning than how the people of Israel got through the Red Sea."

Disagreement over Bible Translations

Older Builders usually appreciate the formality and beauty of the King James Version of the Bible. Younger Builders and most Boomers and Busters want to use translations that are written in modern English, which is easier to understand. It's difficult for everyone in a church to agree to use one translation, so they all bring their personal favorites. This can be a problem for congregational reading of the Bible. The best solution is to print the Scripture to be read in the program so everyone has the same version.

Differing Views of the Church

Builders know that the church is really the people and not the building, but in practice they think of it as God's house, and they can be emotionally attached to the church structure. In many cases it took a lot of sacrifice and money to build the structure, and Builders want to protect it. They may object to coffee in the sanctuary and the youth using the fellowship hall.

Boomers and Busters do not view the church building as sacred in any way. To them the facility is there to be used for ministry. So coffee is allowed in the sanctuary, and it's fine for the children to play Nerfball soccer in the fellowship hall.

As far as management of the church is concerned, Builders want to know what's going on. They attend business meetings to check up on the pastors and church leaders. Most Boomers and Busters seem willing to give leaders responsibility and authority and to trust them to act wisely. Builders like to vote on every issue, including what color to paint the church kitchen. Boomers and Busters are willing to leave such decisions up to the leaders.

Annoyance over Church Attendance

Most Builders were raised during the one-breadwinner system. When the mother didn't work outside the home, there was more time for church participation and volunteerism. It was not unusual for the family to spend several evenings a week at church activities. A strong commitment to Christ was and is played out in a strong commitment to church attendance.

Boomers and Busters are either partners in or children of a dual-income family. The pressure of both parents working outside the home leaves much less time to go to church. They will often be too tired to attend church in the evening and will decide to stay home and spend time together. Their strong commitment to Christ is played out in commitment to their relationships.

Misunderstood Priorities

Builders have placed a priority on foreign missions. Participation in two world wars convinced Builders that sin was real. They saw it face-to-face, especially as they freed the death camp survivors in Germany. The growing economy of the 1950s provided the necessary income to support foreign missions, and the general philosophy of ministry developed that a church that supported foreign missions would grow and one that did not would fail.

Boomers found that their efforts to change the world were not very successful. They tried to bring about world peace and break down racial barriers. To some extent they've seen changes, but they've found that the greatest successes come when working on problems in the local community. Thus they tend to focus on missions close to home. Busters, too, find it difficult to be involved in a mission by simply giving money towards it. They want to *do* something, so they become involved in local projects. Boomers and Busters often feel that Builders were wrong to stress foreign missions while neglecting the families and problems in their own neighborhoods.

Struggle over Pastoral Care

Builders see pastoral care as the responsibility of the paid pastoral staff, particularly the senior pastor. Boomers and

Busters want to practice the "one anothers" of Scripture and care for each other.

Builders expect to be visited. Boomers and Busters are often surprised by and even uncomfortable with a visit. They would rather "do lunch" or meet for breakfast.

Disunity over the Use of Drama and Video

Builders are used to having everything in print, from songs in a hymnal to announcements in the bulletin. They are uncomfortable with information in church being delivered through video and drama.

Boomers and Busters are very comfortable with all audiovisual media, which have been a part of their lives for as long as they can remember. It seems appropriate to use audiovisuals in church because they can help clarify the message.

Contention over Programs

Builders experienced the success of traditional programs like the Sunday evening worship service, midweek prayer meeting, and Sunday school. They remember times when these services and programs were the foundation of the church.

Time-pressed Busters and Boomers see some of these traditional programs and services as ineffective time wasters and would like to see them canceled or at least restructured into more effective formats.

Builders are especially nostalgic about the Sunday school. Many remember being taken to Sunday school by their parents. Prior to the 1950s Sunday schools tended to be evangelistic, and numerous Builders received the Lord as their Savior while attending. Builders are critical of small groups if time is spent only in fellowship and not in Bible study. Many resist the personal sharing so common in small groups.

Most Busters and many Boomers see Sunday school as a boring time primarily geared to children. Following World War II, the goal of most Sunday schools has been education rather than evangelism. The content-orientation of most Sunday schools today is contrary to what Boomers and Busters are looking for—relationships. They prefer small group meetings where they can get to know people, open up, share their hurts, and receive support. They do not think the traditional Sunday school can meet those needs.

Five New Models

For churches that desire to minister in our changing generational scene, there are five primary models being used today.

The Blended Model

Blended churches are those which combine two or more differing philosophies of ministry, usually in the worship service. This commonly used model was described in chapter 10. Churches using this model are characterized by

- two styles of music in one worship service
- traditional ministries and new ones side-by-side
- changing terminology
- a transitional atmosphere
- continuing tension over the philosophy of ministry

The Seeker Model

Seeker churches are those that target their ministries, particularly their outreach ministries, to the unchurched. There are two types of seeker models: seeker driven and seeker sensitive. In the seeker-driven model, the Sunday morning worship service is planned solely to target the unchurched individual. In the seeker-sensitive model the Sunday morning worship service is planned to meet the needs of the believer but with great sensitivity to the unchurched person who may attend. This model of ministry is the second most popular, particularly as new church plants. They tend to be

- driven by demographic research
- targeted to unchurched Boomers and Busters
- focused on felt needs
- geared to evangelism
- committed to having a neutral sounding church name

The Multiple-Track Model

Multiple-track churches are those that offer distinct approaches to ministry at different times, particularly in two or more worship services. This model of ministry is the reverse of the blended model and is quite popular among churches with large contingencies of different generations. It allows the use of two distinct philosophies of ministry at the same time. Churches using this model tend to

- offer different styles of worship
- offer separate ministries for each generation
- allow for lots of diversity
- provide ways for the generations to minister to each other
- reach multiple target groups

The Satellite Model

Churches using this model are those that have one or more worship services in different geographical locations. This model is not as well known or as popular as the first three due to the logistical difficulties involved in making it work. Churches using this model

- are extremely healthy
- are committed to evangelize a different generation
- are not afraid to take risks
- have a senior pastor with a long tenure
- have the talent and management skills to pull it off

The Rebirthed Model

Rebirthed churches are those that completely stop using one philosophy of ministry and begin using a new philosophy. There are very few churches using this model in the United States, but many smaller churches should give it serious consideration in the future. Usually churches using this model

- are very small
- face a major loss of attendance, funds, and ministry effectiveness
- have a core of people who have a vision for a new style of church
- have a pastor with the same new vision and, in some cases, a church planting background
- have a sense of desperation

Conclusion

For church leaders who find themselves dealing with the problems caused by the collision of changing generations in their churches, the best advice is to be open to change. If we struggle and try to fight our way back to the way things used to be, we will expend a lot of useless energy and may drown in our own efforts. Instead of fighting, we need to relax and go with the flow, seeking to understand what is taking place. Later there will be time to adjust to the flow and develop a model of ministry that is just right for the congregation. I'm not talking about doctrinal or spiritual compromise. If we get caught in the flow of doctrinal error, we must fight it with all the energy we have. But in reference to the functional changes taking place in our churches, we need to take a wise approach. We should be willing to use whatever methods or models work best, without compromising our message or integrity.

12

Wave Runners

Anyone who has watched people on water skis has observed skiers crisscrossing and hopping over the wake created by the boat that is pulling them along. Jumping the small wakes created by boats appears to be easily done. Water skiers master the technique quite easily, and they always seem to have fun doing it.

One of the most popular innovations in water recreation has been the development of Jet Skis or Sea-doos. These small water vehicles allow the driver to sit, kneel, or stand up while he jets around a lake or ocean, much like water skiers, but without the necessity of a towing boat. In lakes it is common to see these Jet Skis running over the wakes created by boats or other Jet Skis. But in the ocean, where the waves are much larger, it becomes more of a challenge. Still the people running the waves appear to have great fun. Occasionally one of these wave runners will attempt a jump over a much larger wave or perhaps try to cross one at a wrong angle. When this happens the craft often capsizes, throwing the rider off. Fortunately the manufacturers of these water vehicles thought about this and built in a device that causes the Jet Ski to stay in one place and simply move around in circles. This allows the rider time to swim back to the Jet Ski and continue with his fun.

Wave running over the wakes created by changing generations in a local church can be as much fun as running waves in a lake. At other times, it can be disastrous. Sometimes the wakes caused by generational change are fairly small. Other times they are the overwhelming waves of the ocean. Occasionally they become tidal waves, too powerful for anyone to jump.

As wave runners in our churches, we need to be aware of the generational changes taking place and structure a plan to effectively run the waves of change.

Implications for the Future

We actually know very little about change and what we know is changing, but we can be sure that the future is going to be different from the past. Take television, for instance. Television began in 1939. The battery-powered television came in 1950. In 1956 the first portable black-and-white sets were introduced. NBC began broadcasting all programs in color in 1966. By the early 1980s, 98 percent of all homes in the United States owned at least one T.V. set, some even more. Today we have HDTV (high-definition television), and some predict that we will soon have hologram televisions where three-dimensional figures act out scenes on our living-room floors.

The point is, nothing is staying the same. Times change and so do the generations. Here are a few selected implications for churches as the generational waves flow through them.

The Builder Wave

Studies show that we all think of ourselves as fifteen years younger than we actually are.[1] So members of the Builder Generation may be younger, at least in their hearts, than we think. However, the ability of the Builder Generation to carry on programs and projects will wane as they grow older.

Builders will continue to support the church financially until retirement. After that, it will depend on their disposable income and other factors. As loyal followers they will certainly continue to give sacrificially, as they always have done. When he was getting ready to build a new church facility, Pastor Doug Murren of Eastside Foursquare Church in Kirkland, Washington, discovered who gives the most money. He writes, "First, I found in preparing to build a new facility that at least 80 percent of funding for Christian organizations comes from people 55 and older."[2] With this in mind, church leaders must begin now to educate Boomers about financial stewardship. If we do not, we can surely expect the financial giving to churches to go down.

Revivalistic evangelism styles will continue to decline along with the Builder Generation. This style of evangelism rose to popularity during a time when people needed entertainment as well as the Lord. Builders brought their friends to church so that the preacher could win them to Christ. It was a ministry style that worked well at one time but not so well anymore. People do not need the church for entertainment any more, but they still need the Lord. Now evangelism is best done through a friendship approach, rather than a program approach.

Loyalty to institutions will continue to decline along with the Builder Generation. The two generations following on the heels of the Builders have not seen much in government, savings and loans, or other institutions to raise their trust level. We will need to win the loyalty of Boomers and

Busters one-by-one through excellent service and culturally relevant ministry.

The Boomer Wave

As the Builders gradually move out of the leadership of existing churches, it is likely that a number of church programs will be dropped. The Boomers support people-oriented programs, and as they come into leadership, they will evaluate old ministries against this value. Programs and projects that can show they are honestly making a difference in people's lives will be kept; those that cannot will most likely be discontinued.

Financial stewardship will be related to people projects and vision. One thing for sure, Boomers do not give their money to pay bills. They give it to support vision. Boomers can never get away from the sixties when they poured their lives into big concerns like civil rights. Churches that give Boomers a big vision will get their time, their money, and their emotional support. Thankfully we have the "cause of all causes," but we must learn to communicate it with passion and in the language of today if we want to attract the Boomers' commitment.

Friendship evangelism will continue strong for the Boomer Generation. Unchurched Boomers will be open to hearing the gospel from their friends, so the sharing of testimonies and the gospel will need to take place within the network of relationships. "Let's do lunch" will be received better than "Come to the men's breakfast on Saturday morning."

Loyalty to people will be the prime motivator for Boomers in the church. The ministries that are likely to survive are ones that are built around relationships. Ministries that are casual and flexible and that operate with a simple structure will be popular.

The Buster Wave

It will take some time, but gradually Busters will help churches become involved in issue-oriented projects. No other generation has had as much concern for the environment, and as they have opportunity, they will prick the conscience of the church on that and similar issues. Busters will call the church back to some of its traditional values such as respect for family. But churches will need to become more flexible as this diverse group enters into leadership.

Busters will not be large givers to our churches for many years. They are now either still in school or just getting started in their jobs. It will be some time before they reach their peak earning years. Emotionally they will be drawn to give financially to issues and causes close to home. Like the Boomers they also will be inclined to give to projects that prove their worth by ministering effectively to people.

Friendship evangelism will work with Busters, but it will be twelve-step programs and support-group evangelism events that lead the way. As the most hurting generation to come our way in some time, they have many internal needs that will have to be met. Churches that wish to reach unchurched Busters must invest money, leadership, and personal commitment to support-group projects. Churches effectively reaching Busters will focus much of their ministry in their own area rather than around the globe.

Prepare to Run Some Waves

Running the waves of generational change means we must restructure our ministries so they fit the newer generations. Starting new ministries, restructuring older ones, or eliminating previously successful programs is difficult in any situation but can be a major wave to jump in a multigenerational church. The following steps are a composite of ideas suggested by those who have run the generational waves before us.

1. Bless the past. When I left my church in 1983 to enter the field of church consulting, the church called Dr. Don Weaver to be the pastor. Due to the fact that I was traveling quite a bit and that we had deep roots in the church, Don asked my family to keep attending the church, which we did. On the occasional Sundays that I was there I was often amazed to hear Pastor Don affirm my ministry publicly before the congregation. He did not do this just to impress me because people told me he did it when I wasn't there. I noticed that whenever he publicly affirmed my wife and me, the audience would nod their heads in agreement. And, the more he affirmed us, the more the people loved him and trusted him.

Unless you are a church planter, you will be building on the foundation of others. It was their commitment, sacrifice, and love for the Lord that brought your church to where it is today. Always pay respect and honor to the past leaders and pastors who have served faithfully over the years. If you do so, the congregation will grow in its love for you and your ministry.

2. Affirm the validity of previous methods and programs. Over the years priorities and needs change. Some old ministries lose their effectiveness while new ones are born. As an example, take Vacation Bible School. In the 1950s VBS was a very effective way to reach children during the summer months. Almost every church had some form of this ministry. But, as far as I am aware, almost no churches had a divorce recovery group in the 1950s. Today, it is almost the reverse. The numerous activities available for children in the 1990s have lowered the effectiveness of VBS, and many churches have stopped using it. But new churches add divorce recovery groups every day.

Learn what ministries are legendary in the history of your church and begin to affirm them and the people who served in them. This is particularly important to do with ministries that you are planning to restructure or replace. Let your people know that you understand the place the ministry holds in your church and in their hearts.

3. *Highlight the biblical principles that underlie the previous methods.* Methods and programs are not long-term but the foundational principles that created and supported them are. As you affirm the past leaders and ministries, highlight the foundational principles that undergirded them. For example, a foundational principle that undergirded VBS was evangelism. So, as you affirm VBS, highlight the church's commitment to evangelism. Think through each ministry that will need to be changed and identify the biblical principles that made it valid. Teach and preach the Scripture, the values, and basic principles that are timeless and remain valid today.

4. *Present your new approach as an extension of the past.* Building on the first three steps just noted, present your new approach to ministry as an extension of the former ministry. For example, if your desire is to begin a blended worship service, do not present it as a replacement for a poor worship service that is not meeting needs. Instead, focus on the fact that you are just expanding your already good service so that it will reach more people.

5. *Illustrate how the new approach carries on the values of the former ministry.* One church I worked with in 1986 wanted to move away from a midweek prayer meeting and Bible study and institute a small group ministry that would meet several nights a week. In the process of obtaining the congregation's ownership in the new small group ministry, the pastor and church leaders spent a great deal of time helping the people see that the purpose (value) of the midweek meeting was prayer. They highlighted how the early found-

ers of the church believed that prayer was the main foundation for church effectiveness, and that they were correct. Gradually the church leaders demonstrated to the congregation that the new small group ministry was just building on the founders' commitments and that, in fact, more people would be praying if there were several small groups meeting at different times during the week. The congregation agreed to give it a try, and within one month attendance at the small groups tripled that of the one midweek service.

6. Assure people that you will be carrying on the tried and true biblical principles of old. Take time to educate people so that they understand it is the form of the ministry that is changing but not the foundation. Stress the principles of 1 Corinthians 9:19–23 and show how your new ministry is becoming "all things to all men so that you might win some." Keep stressing the biblical principles of the past more than the styles of the past, bridging into an explanation of how the newer styles carry on the old principles.

7. Listen and love. If the change is major—changing to two worship services or becoming blended—take a minimum of one year to work through the above steps. Leaders of multigenerational churches need to give people time to share their feelings, vent their frustrations, and become accustomed to the new ways of ministry. It is wise to provide small forums where a few people can ask questions rather than have a full congregational meeting. Be willing to meet with some people individually as needed to hear their concerns. Much of the time they just want to be assured that they will not be forgotten.

8. Communicate that traditions are honored best when they are carried on in new ministries. There are dead traditions and living traditions. Communion is a living tradition because it points us to the past and the future. It causes us to remember the Lord's sacrifice on our behalf and, at the same time, calls us to look for his coming in hope.

Dead traditions continue to be remembered but have little impact on life and people today. But living traditions continue on by providing the historical reason for ministries that are being accomplished today. The best traditions are the ones that point to the future through effective ministries that reach people today.

9. Be patient. Understand that in urban and suburban areas of the United States, it normally takes five to seven years to turn an existing church in a new direction. In more rural settings it often takes ten to twelve years and sometimes longer. Church leaders who are going through a time of generational change should be careful to take the long view. While we may not be able to accomplish as much this year as we might hope, we will accomplish more over the next five years than we think.

10. Trust God to make a way for it all to happen. The old hymn says it well, "O God, our help in ages past, our hope for years to come." What better words to bear in mind while leading a multigenerational church. As we love God and his people, he will help us lead them to effectively minister to all three generations.

Value Each Other

Whatever the issues, a major role for wave runners is to encourage mutual respect between generations. Throughout the Book of Proverbs younger generations are told to listen to the counsel of the older generation. Older generations, though, should focus on the inherent values of Scripture rather than on the personal habits or stylistic differences the younger generations adopt. Scriptural values such as honesty, overcoming temptations, wise use of the tongue, and putting God first are values all generations need to hear.

There is not much written in Scripture regarding the older generation's respect for the younger. However some insights might be gained from a study of such passages like, "Fathers, do not exasperate your children, that they may not lose heart" (Col. 3:21); and "Fathers, do not provoke your children to anger; but bring them up in the discipline and instruction of the Lord" (Eph. 6:4). From a generational perspective the older generation must be careful not to exasperate or provoke the younger generations. Otherwise they may "lose heart" for the church and for Christ.

Dr. Larry Regenfuss of South Tacoma Baptist Church in Tacoma, Washington, suggests a seven-step plan for cross-generational cooperation as outlined in Romans 12:10–18.

Step one: Be devoted to one another in brotherly love.
Step two: Give preference to one another in honor.
Step three: Be of the same mind toward one another.
Step four: Do not be haughty in mind.
Step five: Do not be wise in your own estimation.
Step six: Respect what is right in the sight of all men.
Step seven: Be at peace with all men.[3]

Conclusion

F. W. Woolworth Company, one of the last great American five-and-dime retail stores, is in trouble. As a pioneer of the new marketing concept of see-and-touch merchandising in 1879, it was amazingly successful. So much so that in 1913 its founder Frank Woolworth built a skyscraper in New York City as his headquarters and paid for it in cash.

Eventually there were Woolworth stores everywhere, but in 1993 almost half of the remaining 800 stores were scheduled for closure. Woolworth's problems are partly due to our struggling economy. Its major problem, however, is that it has not been able to let go of the past.

Frank Woolworth, who died in 1919, looked to the future and allowed his five-and-dime to change with the times. In 1912 he merged his smaller single stores into a major chain, which positioned him as a giant for years to come. The sad thing is the generations that have followed him at Woolworth were not able to ride the changes as well as he did.[4]

Running waves on water skis, a Jet Ski, or a Sea-doo is not as easy as it looks. When riders first take to the waves, they usually end up in the water quite a number of times before they get the hang of it. As generational wave runners we may occasionally find ourselves in the water, and it may be hot rather than cold. But once we get the hang of it we will find that it is challenging and exciting. Come on now, get on your skis and start running some waves.

Notes

Waves of Change

1. Some authors identify four generations by dividing the Builders in two or by adding Boomer grandchildren as an additional one. Readers who are seriously interested in an in-depth analysis of various generations should read the massive book *Generations: The History of America's Future 1584 to 2069* by William Strauss and Neil Howe published by Quill in 1991. For purposes of simplicity, I will look at the Builders as one large generation.

2. Bill Nichols, "Democrats See Team As a 'Contrast'" *USA Today* (July 10–12, 1992).

3. For two recent studies on church size, see Carl F. George, *How to Break Growth Barriers* (Grand Rapids: Baker Book House, 1993) and George Barna, *Today's Pastors* (Ventura: Regal Books, 1993).

4. Carla Wheeler, "Megachurches," *The San Bernardino Sun,* July 18, 1993, E.

5. Quoted by Lyle E. Schaller in "Whatever Happened to the Baby Boomers?" *The Journal of the Minister's Personal Library*, vol. VI, no. 1 (1985).

6. For information contact ACMC, P.O. Box ACMC, Wheaton, IL 60189-8000. Phone 708-260-1660.

7. Quoted in *Communication Briefings,* vol. 4, no. 2 (n.d.). For further information, write Fund-Raising Institute Monthly Portfolio, Box 365, Ambler, PA 19002.

Chapter 1: What Shaped the Builders?

1. Douglas Alan Walrath, *Frameworks: Patterns of Living and Believing Today* (New York: Pilgrim Press, 1987).

2. Technically groups of people who share common frames of reference are called cohorts. A cohort is composed of those who share experiences that uniquely and fundamentally shape them. A cohort may or may not be a complete generation. Indeed there may be several different cohorts within a generational group. Since for the purposes of this book I am speaking in broad terms, I will not deal with individual cohorts.

3. Trent Christman quoted by Grant Dillman, "Military Broadcasters Are Four Wars Old," *Senior Highlights* (March 1993), 5.

4. Win Arn and Charles Arn, *Live Long and Love It* (Wheaton: Tyndale House Publishers, Inc., 1991), 6.

5. Statistics reported in *L.I.F.E. LINE*, newsletter of the International L.I.F.E. Organization, no. 17 (n.d.), 3.

Chapter 2: Builders and the Church

1. Edmund Fuller, ed., *2,500 Anecdotes for All Occasions* (New York: Avenel, 1970), 119.

2. Win Arn, *The Win Arn Growth Report,* no. 26 (1989), 4.

3. Donald E. Anderson, *Retire or Refire? Goals for the Final Lap from Philippians,* unpublished dissertation at Talbot School of Theology (1990), 24–25.

4. Frank Minirth, John Reed, and Paul Meier, *Beating the Clock: A Guide to Maturing Successfully* (Grand Rapids: Baker Book House, 1985), 13.

5. J. William Mason and Lillian Mason, *You Can Be Happy Though Retired* (Dallas: Crescendo, 1979), 107.

6. Auren Uris, *Over 50: The Definitive Guide to Retirement* (Radnor, Penn.: Chilton, 1979), 11.

7. Quoted by James B. Gaffney, "Grandparents Raising Grandkids, Tough Going in the '90s," *Colorado Springs Senior Beacon*, July 1992, A16.

8. Anderson, *Retire or Refire?* 14–15.

9. Arn, *The Win Arn Growth Report,* 2.

10. Reported by Dr. Mark D. Hayward, associate professor of sociology at Penn State and director of the Gerontology Center.

11. Paul Faulkner, *Making Things Right When Things Go Wrong: Ten Proven Ways to Put Your Life in Order* (Fort Worth: Sweet, 1986), 83.

Chapter 3: Elderly Builders

1. Patrick J. Morris, "Elder Power," *The San Bernardino Sun,* July 1, 1990, D1.

2. Reported in the *Gallup Poll Monthly* (January 1990), 19.

3. Win Arn, "The Church's Challenge and Opportunity of an Aging America . . . ," *The Win Arn Growth Report,* no. 26 (1989).

4. Reported in "Malnutrition among Elders Called Alarming by Experts," in the Riverside/San Bernardino edition of *Senior World,* January 1993, 26.

5. Quoted in "The Center for Aging Resources—Reaching Out to a Graying Population," *Fuller Focus* (Fall 1992), 6. For information call the Center for Aging Resources at (818) 577-8480.

6. "The Center for Aging Resources," 5.

7. "Family Ties Mean More in Times of Crisis, Study Says," Riverside/San Bernardino edition of *Senior World,* January 1993, 27.

8. "Caregivers to Elderly Should Watch Out for Stress, Burnout," *The San Bernardino Sun,* August 17, 1991.

9. "Widows Adjust to Being Alone," Riverside/San Bernardino edition of *Senior World,* September 1992, 29.

10. See the author's book *Finding Them, Keeping Them* (Nashville: Broadman/Holman Press, 1992) for ideas on how to develop "presence ministries" in a church.

Chapter 4: Who Are the Boomers?

1. Walrath, *Frameworks.*

2. For a detailed explanation of the differences between the early and later Boomer cohorts, the reader should see Cheryl Russell, *100 Predictions for the Baby Boom* (New York: Plenum Press, 1987), 41–46.

3. Alice Kahn, "Hey Hey, They're the Boomers," *San Francisco Chronicle,* March 18, 1992, C1.

4. Quoted by Janet Cawley, "Baby Boomers Ready to Accept Torch," *Chicago Tribune,* September 20, 1992, City edition, 18.

5. Quoted by Cawley, "Baby Boomers Ready to Accept Torch," 18.

6. Russell, *100 Predictions for the Baby Boom,* 32–33.

7. Irving Kristol, *Reflections of a NeoConservative* (New York: Basic Books, 1983), 27.

8. "Here Come the Baby-Boomers," *U.S. News & World Report* (November 5, 1984), 68.

9. Russell, *100 Predictions for the Baby Boom,* 40.

10. Janet Cawley, quoting Paul Light of the Hubert H. Humphrey Institute at the University of Minnesota, 19.

11. Susan Mitchell, "Rock and Roll Will Never Die," *The Boomer Report* 5, no. 6 (June 15, 1993), 7.

12. Feliz Satir, "Is It Time for a Job Change?" *The San Bernardino Sun,* May 17, 1992, G1.

13. Phil Goodman, "Radio Still Reaches the Boomers," *The Boomer Report* 5, no. 6 (June 15, 1993), 7.

Chapter 5: Boomer Believers

1. Elmer L. Towns, "Reaching the Baby Boomer," *Church Growth Today* 5, no. 5 (1990), 1.

2. Lyle E. Schaller, "Whatever Happened to the Baby Boomers?" *Newsletter* (1985), 9.

3. Quoted by Peter Steinfels, "Charting the Currents of Belief for the Generation That Rebelled," *The New York Times,* May 30, 1993.

4. Reported in *The Church Around the World,* Tyndale House Newsletter (October 1992), 2.

5. Quoted by Steinfels, "Charting the Currents."

6. Leith C. Anderson, "A Senior Pastor's Perspective on Baby Boomers," *Christian Education Journal* XI, no. 1 (Autumn 1990), 75.

7. James Scudder, "Renewed Search for Faith," *The San Bernardino Sun,* February 10, 1990, D4.

8. Scudder, "Renewed Search for Faith," D4.

9. For further insight on the case of Boomers returning to the church see George Barna, "The Case of the Mission Boomers," *Ministry Currents* II, no. 1 (January–March, 1992), 1–4.

10. Kenneth Briggs, "Baby Boomers: Boom or Bust for the Churches?" *Progressions,* A Lilly Endowment Occasional Report 2, no. 1 (January 1990), 7.

11. Quoted in "Successfully Reaching Baby Boomers," *MANDATE: A Home Missions Magazine for the Wesleyan Church* (Indianapolis: The Wesleyan Church), 15.

12. Reported in the *Inland Empire Business Journal* (May 1993), 32. For more detailed information see the May 1993 issue of *Working Woman.*

13. James F. Engel, "We Are the World," *Christianity Today* (September 24, 1990), 33.

14. Mike Bellah, *Baby Boom Believers* (Wheaton: Tyndale House, 1988), 129.

Chapter 6: Reaching the Boomer Generation

1. For more information contact: AAB, 2621 W. Airport Freeway, No. 105, Irving, TX 75062.

2. Walter Hatch, "Election Analysts See 'Baby Boom' Voters' Influence," *Seattle Times* (November 12, 1989).

3. Charles W. Colson, "A Call to Rescue the Yuppies," *Christianity Today* (May 17, 1985), 20.

4. Quoted by Jeannye Thornton, "Those City Lights," *U.S. News & World Report* (March 4, 1985), 61.

5. For complete details see Wade Clark Roof, *A Generation of Seekers: The Spiritual Journeys of the Baby Boom Generation* (New York: HarperCollins Publishers, 1993).

6. Don Lattin, "Fast-track Baby Boomers Slow for God," *The San Bernardino Sun,* November 25, 1989, religion section.

7. Quoted in "Staying on the Marriage Track in the 1990s," *USA Today* (March 1990), 10.

8. Quoted by Walter Shapiro, "The Birth and—Maybe—Death of Yuppiedom," *Time* (April 8, 1991), 65.

9. Quoted by Joan Smith, "Let Us Pray," *The San Francisco Examiner,* June 6, 1993, D5.

10. Reported by John Case, "The Real Age Wave," *INC* (July 1989), 23.

11. Bellah, *Baby Boom Believers,* 32–33.

12. Reported in "Which Way to Retirement?" (TIAA-CREF, P.O. Box 2156, New York, NY 10163, 1993), 2.

13. Quoted by Peter Steinfels, "Charting the Currents of Belief for the Generation That Rebelled," *New York Times,* May 30, 1993.

14. Quoted in "Successfully Reaching Baby Boomers," *MANDATE: A Home Missions Magazine for the Wesleyan Church* (Indianapolis: The Wesleyan Church, Spring 1991), 15.

15. Elmer Towns, "How to Reach the Baby Boomer," a seminar presented by the Church Growth Institute, P.O. Box 4404, Lynchburg, VA 24502 (January 1990).

Chapter 7: Why Are They Called Busters?

1. "Simpsons Help Save a Life," *The San Bernardino Sun,* May 25, 1992, D6.

2. Bill Marvel and Melissa Morrison, "The Pacifier People," *The Dallas Morning News,* February 7, 1993, F1.

3. George Shultz, quoted by Richard Saul Wurman, *Information Anxiety* (New York: Doubleday, 1989), 41, 309.

4. Marvel and Morrison, "The Pacifier People," F1.
5. Marvel and Morrison, "The Pacifier People," F4.
6. David M. Gross and Sophfronia Scott, "Proceeding with Caution," *Time* (July 16, 1990), 58.
7. Alan Deutschman, "What 25-Year-Olds Want," *Fortune* (August 27, 1990), 43.

Chapter 8: Busters and the Church

1. Marvel and Morrison, "The Pacifier People," F4.
2. Alice Kahn and Shann Nix, "Who's Stressed and Who's Blessed," *San Francisco Chronicle,* July 12, 1993.

Chapter 9: Reaching Busters

1. Clark Morphew, "Bringing 'Buster' Generation to Religion," *The Press-Enterprise* (March 6, 1993).
2. Helaine Olen, "Women Say They'll Put Family First," *L.A. Times,* Orange County edition.

Chapter 10: Blending Generations

1. "2,024 sq. ft. Showcase Home Built by Consumer Research," *The San Bernardino Sun,* May 26, 1993, A7.
2. Portions of this chapter originally appeared in the McIntosh *Church Growth Network Newsletter,* vol. 1, no. 7 (1989).

Chapter 12: Wave Runners

1. Eric Sevareid, "A New Stage," *Modern Maturity* (April–May 1991), 73.
2. Douglas Murren, "Reaching Boomers," *Ministries Today* (January–February 1989).
3. Larry Regenfuss, "What Do You Mean, 'Common Sense'?" an unpublished research paper (January 1990), 41–42.
4. Adapted from Arnold Garson, "Woolworth Should Have Changed with Times," *The San Bernardino Sun,* October 17, 1993, D.

Resources

General

Anderson, Leith. *Dying for Change.* Minneapolis: Bethany House, 1990.

Bloom, Allan. *The Closing of the American Mind.* New York: Simon & Schuster, 1987.

Chandler, Russell. *Racing toward 2001.* Grand Rapids: Zondervan Publishing House, 1992.

Dychtwald, Ken. *Age Wave.* Los Angeles: Jeremy P. Tarcher, Inc., 1989.

Gerber, Jerry, et al. *Life-Trends: Your Future for the Next 30 Years.* New York: Avon Books, 1991.

Lasch, Christopher. *The Culture of Narcissism.* New York: Warner Communications Co., 1979.

McIntosh, Gary L., and Glen S. Martin. *The Issachar Factor: Understanding the Trends Confronting Your Church and Designing a Strategy for Success.* Nashville: Broadman/Holman, 1994.

Postman, Neil. *Amusing Ourselves to Death.* New York: Elisabeth Sifton Books, 1985.

Strauss, William, and Neil Howe. *Generations: The History of America's Future 1584 to 2069.* New York: Quill, 1991.

Toffler, Alvin. *Previews and Premises.* New York: Random House, 1983.

Walrath, Douglas Alan. *Frameworks: Patterns of Living and Believing Today.* New York: Pilgrim Press, 1987.

Wattenberg, Ben J. *The Birth Dearth.* New York: Pharos Books, 1987.

The Builder Wave

Anderson, Don. *Keep the Fire!* Sisters, Ore.: Multnomah Books, 1994.

Arn, Win, and Charles Arn. *Live Long and Love It!* Wheaton: Tyndale House Publishers, Inc., 1991.

L.I.F.E. LINE, the newsletter of the International L.I.F.E. Organization, 1857 Highland Oaks, Arcadia, CA 91006 (818-355-2470)

Mason, J. William, and Lillian Mason. *You Can Be Happy Though Retired.* Dallas: Crescendo, 1979.

Minirth, Frank, John Reed, and Paul Meier. *Beating the Clock: A Guide to Maturing Successfully.* Grand Rapids: Baker Book House, 1985.

Modern Maturity Magazine, 3200 E. Carson St., Lakewood, CA 90712.

Uris, Auren. *Over 50: The Definitive Guide to Retirement.* Radnor, Penn.: Chilton, 1979.

The Boomer Wave

Bast, Robert L. *The Missing Generation.* Monrovia, Calif.: Church Growth, Inc., 1991.

Bellah, Mike. *Baby Boom Believers.* Wheaton: Tyndale House Publishers, Inc., 1988.

Boutilier, Robert. *Targeting Families: Marketing to and through the New Family.* Ithaca, N.Y.: American Demographics, 1993.

Collins, Gary R., and Timothy E. Clinton. *Baby Boomer Blues.* Dallas: Word Publishing, 1992.

Engel, James F., and Jerry D. Jones. *Baby Boomers and the Future of World Missions.* Orange, Calif.: Management Development, 1989.

Francese, Peter, and John Naisbitt. *The Expert's Guide to the Baby Boomers.* New York: Time, Inc.

Frinzel, Hans. *Help! I'm a Baby Boomer.* Wheaton: Victor Books, 1989.

Jones, Landen Y. *Great Expectations.* New York: Coward, McCann, and Geophegan, 1980.

Light, Paul C. *Baby Boomers.* New York: W. W. Norton & Company, 1988.

Murren, Doug. *The Baby Boomerang.* Ventura, Calif.: Regal Books, 1990.

Nichols, Michael P. *Turning Forty in the Eighties: Personal Crisis, Time for Change.* New York: W. W. Norton, 1986.

Roof, Wade Clark. *A Generation of Seekers.* San Francisco: HarperCollins Publishers, 1993.

Russell, Cheryl. *100 Predictions for the Baby Boom: The Next 50 Years.* New York: Plenum Press, 1987.

———. *The Master Trend: How the Baby Boom Generation Is Reshaping America.* New York: Plenum Press, 1993.

Wallechivsky, David. *Midterm Report: The Class of 1965.* New York: Viking Penguin Press, 1986.

Walrath, Douglas Alan. *Frameworks: Patterns of Living and Believing Today.* New York: Pilgrim Press, 1987.

Wolfe, David B. *Marketing to Boomers and Beyond.* New York: McGraw-Hill, Inc., 1993.

The Buster Wave

Barna, George. *The Invisible Generation: Baby Busters.* Glendale, Calif.: Barna Research Group, Inc., 1992.

Bradford, Lawrence, and Claire Raines. *Twentysomething.* New York: MasterMedia Limited, 1992.

Coupland, Doug. *Generation X: Tales for an Accelerated Culture.* New York: St. Martin's Press, 1991.

Dunn, William. *The Baby Bust: A Generation Comes of Age.* Ithaca, N.Y.: American Demographics, 1993.

Gerber, Jerry, Janet Wolff, Walter Klores, and Gene Brown. *Life-Trends.* New York: Avon Books, 1989.

Gibb, Steven. *Twentysomething, Floundering, and Off the Yuppie Track.* Chicago: The Noble Press, Inc., 1992.

Howe, Neil, and Bill Strauss. *13th GEN: Abort, Retry, Ignore, Fail?* New York: Vintage, 1993.

Ianni, Francis. *The Search for Structure: A Report on American Youth Today.* New York: The Free Press, 1989.

Koons, Carolyn A., and Michael J. Anthony. *Single Adult Passages.* Grand Rapids: Baker Book House, 1991.

Littwin, Susan. *The Postponed Generation.* New York: Quill, 1987.

Loeb, Paul Rogat. *Generation at the Crossroads.* New Brunswick, N.J.: Rutgers University Press, 1994.

Sciacca, Fran. *Generation at Risk.* Chicago: Moody Press, 1990.

Organizations

AARP (American Association of Retired Persons), 1909 K St. NW, Washington, DC 20049 (202) 872-4700

AFL-CIO Dept. of Community Services, 815 16th St. NW, Washington, DC 20006 (202) 637-5189

The Alzheimer's Association (800) 621-0379

American Council of Life Insurance, 1001 Pennsylvania Ave. NW, Washington, DC 20004 (202) 624-2000

Christian Association of Prime Timers (CAP), (800) 443-0227

Foundation for Hospice and Home Care, 519 C St. NE, Washington, DC 20002 (202) 547-6586

Gray Panthers, 1424 16th St., Suite 602, Washington, DC 20036

L.I.F.E. International, 1857 Highland Oaks Dr., Arcadia, CA 91006 (818) 355-2470

The National Alliance for the Mentally Ill, (800) 950-6264

National Council of Senior Citizens, 925 15th St. NW, Washington, DC 20005 (202) 347-8800

National Council on the Aging, 600 Maryland Ave. SW, Washington, DC 20024 (202) 479-1200

National Home Caring Council, 519 C St. NE, Washington, DC 20002 (202) 547-6586

National Institute on Aging, Federal Building, Room 6C12, Bethesda, MD 20892 (301) 496-1752

National Institute on Drug Abuse, Elder Education, P.O. Box 416, Kensington, MD 20740

State commissions on aging. Check your local phone book for information on local senior programs.

For information on support groups near you contact American Self-Help Clearinghouse (201) 625-7101

To locate a "respite-care" program in your area contact The Brookdale Center on Aging, 425 E. 25th St., New York, NY 10010-2590 (212) 481-7670

Refer to the white pages of your phone directory for your Area Agency on Aging.

The McIntosh Church Growth Network

In 1989 Dr. Gary L. McIntosh founded the **Church Growth Network,** a consulting firm that assists churches to reach their greatest effectiveness in finding and keeping new people.

The **Church Growth Network** conducts individual consultation with churches with specialization in the areas of generational change, analysis of church health, and five-year planning.

The popular *Church Growth Network Newsletter* is read by approximately 10,000 pastors and church leaders each month. In a short, highly readable format, the *CGN Newsletter* focuses on issues and answers for leaders of today's churches.

For complete information, please contact Dr. Gary L. McIntosh at

Church Growth Network
3630 Camellia Dr.
San Bernardino, CA 92404
(909) 882-5386